WHAT EXPERTS ARE ~~SAYING ABOUT~~
SOUL SMART

"I have waited years for such a book as this, and will recommend it with great enthusiasm. Soul Smart contains some of the most helpful techniques for learning how to hear our loved ones and friends communicate with us after death and ways in which to enhance that attunement. The Appendices provide helpful avenues to have many personal experiences long after reading the book. You will want to KEEP your copy of Soul Smart and give copies to everyone you know. Susanne Wilson has written an excellent book, her personal experiences woven in throughout, and with great insight. She is not only a good writer but is one of the most remarkable evidential mediums I have ever met."

—Anne Puryear, author of *Stephen Lives: My Son Stephen, His Life, Suicide and Afterlife*

"What kind of person writes the following sentence? 'The spirit community is not "somewhere out there," but in fact is right here with us, in virtually the same space as the Earthly community.' The answer is a special person who has a profound awareness and relationship with the 'spirit world.' Susanne Wilson tells us that 'each person now living has a unique spiritual team of spirit guides, angels, and loved ones in the light.' She tells us that our 'team' is a 'gift from our loving Creator, who knows that Earth is a rough-hewn classroom!' Susanne is as evidential as she is spiritual, and Soul Smart is a delicious mixture of practicality and poetry. This is a thoroughly unique book, serious yet playful, experiential yet useful. Susanne has given all of us—including our respective spirit teams—a precious gift. 'And so it is.'"

—Gary E. Schwartz, PhD, Professor of Psychology, Medicine, Neurology, Psychiatry, and Surgery at the University of Arizona; author of *The Afterlife Experiments, An Atheist in Heaven* (with Paul Davids), and *Super Synchronicity*

"Forty-five years ago, I worked with many suffering and dying adults and children in hospitals. This motivated me to discover a bigger-picture perspective that answered life's toughest questions and challenges. I've learned much about the greater reality of angels, guides, 'departed' loved ones, and the Light, but Susanne's book was a treasure chest of new information and techniques. She answered my biggest questions about the afterlife and how we can optimally interact with those who have passed on, but definitely not passed away. I will read Soul Smart again and use her simple but powerful techniques to improve my life here and now. I recommend that you do the same. Thank you, Susanne, for all the love, courage, and dedication it took to create this wonderfully enlightening book."

—Mark Pitstick, MA, DC; SoulProof.com; SoulPhone.org

"Soul Smart is a well-written, fascinating book with unique insights into how we can communicate with loved ones on the other side of life and descriptions of how they communicate with us. The insights are illustrated with engaging stories and 'Soul Smart tips' that contain guidance about how to connect in meditations, dreams, and quiet moments when the person in spirit is sensed as being near. It will be enjoyable reading for both the reader familiar with afterlife communication and the person newly learning the exciting truth that we can continue active, loving relationships with people now living on the next plane of life. It's a delightful book."

—R. Craig Hogan, Ph.D., author of *Your Eternal Self*

"When the student is ready, Susanne Wilson provides. This gem of a book is your turn-to guide for connecting with your Team of guides and loved ones in spirit. An essential read for those who want to connect across the veil."

—Suzanne Giesemann, evidential medium and author of *Messages of Hope*

Soul SMART

WHAT THE DEAD TEACH US ABOUT SPIRIT COMMUNICATION

SECOND EDITION

SUSANNE J. WILSON

Soul Smart by: Susanne J. Wilson

Publisher's Cataloging-In-Publication Data
(Prepared by The Donohue Group, Inc.)

Names: Wilson, Susanne J.
Title: Soul smart : what the dead teach us about spirit communication / Susanne J. Wilson.
Description:: Phoenix, Arizona
Identifiers: ISBN 978-1-5136-3543-9 | 978-1-5136-3701-3 (ebook)
Subjects: LCSH: Spiritualism. | Spirits. | Mediums.
Classification: LCC BF1261.2 .W55 2017 (print) | LCC BF1261.2 (ebook) | DDC 133.9--dc23

Published by
Half Moon Books, LLC, Carefree, AZ 85377

ISBN: 978-1-5136-3543-9

Printed in the United States of America

table of contents

Foreword i
Introduction iii

Part 1: Understanding the Spirit World

Chapter 1: Soul Smart Principles 3
Chapter 2: One Small Medium 13
Chapter 3: Wake-Up Call 19
Chapter 4: What To Expect When You Die 39
Chapter 5: Life Between Lives 49
Chapter 6: Children In Spirit 57

Part 2: Mediumship For Non-Mediums:
Regular People Connecting With Their Loved Ones In Spirit

Chapter 7: How The Dead Send And Receive Messages 79
Chapter 8: Centering Yourself. 89
Chapter 9: Building Up Your Power 97
Chapter 10: How To Have A Dream Visit. 107
Chapter 11: How To Have A Meditation Visit 111
Chapter 12: Spirit Guides And Guardian Angels 121

Appendices: Meditation Scripts

Appendix A: The Daily Peace 141
Appendix B: Synergy Peace–Manifest Health And Serenity. 143
Appendix C: Crossing The Threshold–Preparation To Meet
With Loved Ones & Guides 149
Appendix D: Guidance Quest–Meet Your Spirit Guide 153
Appendix E: Hereafter Now–Connect With Loved Ones In Spirit 159
Appendix F: Love Lives Forever–Connect With Your Beloved in Spirit 165

I dedicate this book to my husband, Carl, for standing by me when others thought I was throwing my life away to be a medium. Thank you for figuring out life with me. I love you, Mr. Man.

foreword

by Victor and Wendy Zammit

Many people tell us that they would give anything to have a personal experience of direct communication with a loved one in spirit—to have the certainty that they continue to exist and that they are happy and still part of our lives. Susanne Wilson's new book contains detailed information on ways such a connection can be achieved by non-mediums.

Soul Smart is written in easy to understand and engaging language. Susanne begins by taking the reader through the basics of what to expect when you die. She continues with chapters on life in the afterlife and the special provisions made for children in spirit. In the second part of the book Susanne shares discoveries gained from her many years of teaching people to connect with their guides and loved ones. She explains the basics of how the dead send and receive messages, how to center yourself and build up your power and how to have a meditation visit and a dream visit. This section of the book contains practical information that we have not come across elsewhere. The final section of the book contains the scripts of some wonderful meditations that we highly recommend for use on a daily basis.

Susanne is an evidential medium whose ability to gain detailed accurate information we have personally witnessed on many occasions. The information she gives about the afterlife is consistent with that which comes through the most reliable sources. Her vivid descriptions are interspersed with accounts of her own personal experiences and with user-friendly takeaway summaries that she calls "Soul Smart tips."

The layout of the book is crisp and user-friendly with bolded subheadings and key points to make it easier to go back and locate those points—important because this is a book that you will come back to over and over again. It is an ideal book to give to someone who is grieving or who is just beginning to ask questions about what happens when you die. And it also contains enough new information to be used for discussion by groups of developing mediums and spiritual seekers.

Victor and Wendy Zammit, co-authors of *A Lawyer Presents the Evidence for the Afterlife* and *The Friday Afterlife Report*

introduction

DO YOU FEEL IT? A great and deep shift in consciousness is happening now all over the Earth. The spirit community is not "somewhere out there," but, in fact, it is right here with us, in virtually the same space as the Earthly community.

People are talking about raising their vibration. But what does "raising your vibration" really mean? One of my favorite ways to answer that question reminds me of science class when I was in junior high school. I enjoyed the subject of science and listened with rapt attention. When our class learned about atoms, our teacher, Mrs. Flanagan, displayed a glass of water, several ice cubes, and a tea kettle sitting atop a Bunsen burner. Pointing to the glass of water, she explained that water in its liquid form flows easily. The ice cubes represented the dense and heavy state of water in its frozen form because freezing slowed down the vibration rate of the water molecules.

Just then, the tea kettle came to a boil. We watched as steam rose from the tea kettle's nozzle. At its fastest vibration, which was boiling, water flew through the air as steam. Have you ever tried to catch steam, put it in a glass, and drink it? Of course not. That's because once the highest possible vibratory rate is achieved, there is virtually nothing that can slow the rate down ever again.

That is why you are here on Earth now; to learn how to rise to your highest vibration so that nothing can ever really slow you down again. This usually involves monitoring all of your thoughts, words, and actions to ensure that compassion and forgiveness–towards yourself and others–are your top priorities.

No one said it would be easy. That is why each person now living has a unique spiritual team of spirit guides, angels, and beloved people and pets in the light. Your team is a gift from our loving Creator, who knows that Earth is a roughhewn classroom! My hope is that you will use *Soul Smart* to create a closer connection with your own spiritual team. I have never forgotten that lesson from Mrs. Flanagan. Please never forget that you are loved, guided, and supported, always.

And you are never alone!

Susanne J. Wilson
Carefree, Arizona USA

part one

UNDERSTANDING THE
SPIRIT WORLD

—— CHAPTER ONE ——

soul smart principles

WELCOME TO YOUR EXCLUSIVE ticket! You are about to receive a behind-the-scenes tour of what happens backstage in Heaven. In addition, you'll have the opportunity to be empowered to communicate confidently with your own beloved dead.

People tend to view the world in absolutes. Right or wrong. Us or them. Dead or alive. Yet each of us has been dead and alive many times; and because consciousness on the Earth is shifting, the border between the dead and living communities is thinning. In fact, the so-called veil between the living and the spirit worlds is a quantum physical manifestation of our all-too-human belief that we are separate from the Source and from other beings not in bodies. Every being is connected to all others, and never is separate from Source. As the people of Earth begin to raise the vibration of their individual shares of our united consciousness, that veil will one day completely disappear!

We are immortal souls living in bodies for a limited time. But our time living in the dead state is unlimited! The dead community or spirit world is *our* world. Communication between the dead and the living is natural, but still it is not easy. It's normal for you to want to hear directly from your spirit guides and angels and your beloved spirit people and pets, but you don't want to be afraid; you want nothing to scare you. You also want to be certain that whatever happens is real and isn't just your imagination.

Soul Smart *shares many best practices for communicating with your spiritual team. Each person has a team of spirit guides, angels, and beloved spirit people and pets. You will learn about spirit communication from the viewpoint of those who are currently living in the dead community, spirit world, or in Heaven or the Summerland, whichever term you might prefer.*

The techniques and advice presented in this book come directly from the spirit world. They are designed by the spirits for safety, discernment, and compassion. You will:

- see what goes on behind the scenes when the spirits are sending you a sign or a synchronicity;

- glimpse into the Halls of Reunion, where your beloved spirit people are rehearsing how they will enter your dream for a visit;

- understand just what your beloved spirit person or pet did that enabled you to catch a glimpse or sense their presence;

- learn what you can do to receive more and clearer communications;

- identify and communicate with your spiritual team, including your guides and angels;

- establish a greater rapport with your master spirit guide;

- validate that you are not just imagining that you can perceive your guide. He or she really is there!

But, wait a minute! Before you dive into *Soul Smart*, there is something important that I need to tell you. This is the same advice that I give to the intuition development students that I mentor in my videoconference classes. Please be advised that:

Reading this book may cause you to have an increase in spontaneous, wonderful, and positive paranormal experiences. Practicing whatever resonates for you from this book can bring you dream and meditation visits, signs, symbols, and synchronicities from those in the spirit world who cherish and protect you. Start a journal and keep notes! You'll enjoy commemorating signs that you receive, which might include noticing repetitive numbers, receiving coins that seem to appear from nowhere, hearing your special song played at exactly the right moment, or perhaps a special visit from a bird, butterfly, or dragonfly. The list of possibilities is endless.

The word "paranormal" simply means "above the norm." Nowadays it often carries an unfortunate eerie connotation, but I assure you that there is nothing scary, bad, or evil about this book or about the methods that it presents. In fact, my life's work is anathema to everything dark! This book is about compassion, wise discernment, unity, and inner peace.

If you have ever heard me speak, you know that I have a pet peeve about television shows that overdo what I call the "scary-bad-evil" side of the paranormal. Yes, there is a dark side in the spirit world, just as there is a dark side in the living community, but your exposure to darkness can be minimized when you have compassion in your heart and apply common sense and discernment. Would you use an ATM machine late at night if you saw a shady character lurking close by and watching you? Of course not. Your gut feeling would tell you to keep moving and find a safer place.

Soul Smart methods are always safe, provided that you approach spirit communication with a loving heart and good intentions. You have nothing to lose and everything to gain by reading on. Now you have the opportunity to better understand life in the spirit world, raise your vibration, and increase your personal spiritual power.

The simple reason why reading this book may increase your spontaneous and positive experiences with spirit is intention. Never underestimate the power of your intention! Whenever you read a book or attend a seminar with the intention of being open to spiritual growth, you signal to the Universe: *"I am ready to let my light shine more brightly."*

Anyone, from beginners to those at more advanced levels, can benefit.

Whenever I teach at a conference or mentor students in my classes, I start with the basics and build on a solid foundation. Therefore, if parts of this book seem like a review for you, I ask you to skim through those parts anyway, as you may find a slightly different twist. When you come to parts of this book that are new and perhaps surprising, that is because I have held nothing back. This is the information that the spirit world wants the living community to have. The spirits want us to know how hard they work for us and with us! They are eager to teach us how to achieve better communication between our planes of existence.

As an evidential medium, I am continually working to deliver ever more precise details, more evidence, in my readings. I am my own toughest critic. This may surprise you, but I am also a bit of a skeptic. I am the right kind of skeptic, though: an open-minded truth-seeker!

This Soul Smart information comes from my personal experiences with the spirits. I am not a scientist working under laboratory conditions, and I have not used scientific methods. I am a medium who has had this gift since birth, and I have worked for twenty-five years, the last eleven years in earnest, to develop my abilities and discernment.

As a lifelong note-taker, I have spent years writing down what spirit people and higher-vibrational beings, including spirit guides and angels, were telling me. The dead have gone into lots of detail, telling and showing me what their lives were like over there, and I have paid close attention, particularly to those who provided excellent evidential details during readings. Even though they didn't know each other, the details that they've shared about spirit communication and what it's like to be in spirit form have been strikingly similar, whether provided by a Chinese man who passed forty years ago or an American woman who died six months ago. And these details have been verified by my personal spiritual team of very loving high-vibrational beings, some of whom even have a sense of humor. I couldn't do any of this without my team!

My documentation of what spirits teach us about spirit communication, supplemented by my own witness and that of my spiritual team, contains remarkable consistency in the information. They strongly agree about what it is like to be in spirit form and what the spirits need from us for good communication between our worlds.

For a recent example, from the early 1990s up until last year more than three dozen different spirits, each reporting independently, have described for me the processes by which they visit the living in dreams and meditations. I have been there during out-of-body experiences to see it for myself!

I am not asking you to take anything in this book on faith alone. Instead, I am suggesting that when you find an element in this book that resonates, you should try it out and see how well it works for you. And as you apply the Soul Smart methods, please remember that Rome wasn't built in a day. Be patient, joyful, disciplined, and consistent in your efforts to communicate with your spirit guides, angels, and beloved spirit people and pets. Remember, communication between the living and the spirit world is natural, but it still is not easy!

After you read this book, I would suggest that you set aside one day each week to work on Soul Smart techniques. Keep a diary or journal. And each time your efforts bear fruit, please remember to give lots of gratitude on the spot. Shout out a big "Thank you!" Gratitude begets more success.

Please note, too, that all the advice given in this book about communicating with spirit loved ones also applies to connecting

with your beloved spirit pets. Every animal with which we have a loving connection is waiting for us there, now young and healthy. Love truly does not end!

A NOTE TO THE NEWLY BEREAVED

If you are grieving the recent loss of a close loved one, please honor your grief. Express your feelings. Cry. Give yourself time. Accept the fact that you won't get over it, but you will get through it. If you are in the throes of fresh grief, this is not the time to work on developing any new spirit communication skills. Please give yourself time to grieve and to allow the people you trust to help you through it. To be clear, I see no problem with the newly grieving reading this book, but I want you to be aware that new and very deep grief may create a blockage to your receiving messages. Time and patience should dissolve the barrier. Meanwhile, the spirit world and I, as a medium, can assure you that your loved one is doing well, loves you, and continues to be a part of your life.

HOUSEKEEPING

Now for a few details about word choice. The spirits assure me that they are *not* offended when we say the word "dead." As far as they are concerned, there is no reason to substitute a gentler euphemism such as "deceased" or "dearly departed" for them. So, when on occasion I use the word "dead" please know that I mean no offense. And please be aware that when I use the words "God" or "Creator" or "Source" it is with the sincerest reverence but definitely not connected to any religion. I am speaking of the highest vibrational energy of all—an intensely pure love and compassion energy that is never apart from you or me. And for simplicity sake I generally use the masculine pronouns "He" or "Him" for this force. There is no need for us ever to mince words, since the Creator and those we love, who are not now in bodies, already perfectly know our hearts.

Everyone is born with the ability to learn how to communicate with his or her OWN beloved spirit family, friends, and pets. But not everyone is born with genuine mediumship ability, the type required for a life of service by bringing through messages from spirit to OTHER people from their spirit loved ones. Not everyone is born to become an excellent professional medium, just like not everyone will become an excellent nurse, actor, architect, or poet!

Soul Smart is not intended to teach you how to become a professional medium, although it may add to the knowledge base of people who are working as mediums. Mediums are born with the gift, and the gift may be suspected in childhood and lie mostly dormant until a precipitating event causes it to surface. A predisposition to mediumship abilities may even be genetic since it seems to run in families.

Professional mediumship is a calling, but you should know that it is perfectly natural for you to pick up very brief, random spirit messages on occasion, and to pass them along to someone. As the overall vibration of people on Earth shifts higher, increasing numbers are becoming able to do this. But I insist (although some will disagree) that those who can become good, professional, evidential mediums are born with a gift, and, at some point, they feel a calling. They begin then to work hard and to nurture their gift.

Please don't try to do this for a living unless you have been studying with a teacher who says you are ready! Professional mediums must consistently deliver clear, accurate, healing messages from spirit for a sustained period of thirty to sixty minutes to clients who are total strangers. It is much harder work than it appears to be! Most mediums can do only one to three readings in a day, and they can't do readings more than a few days per week without risk of becoming ill. As the saying goes, "You can't fill the cup of another if your own cup is empty." Practicing public mediumship is hard work, and only the top one-half percent of mediums ever make much money at it. This book isn't about turning everybody into professional mediums, although it can certainly help those who are working as mediums. My intention is to help you to develop better communication with your own spiritual team: your spirit guides, angels, and beloved spirit people and pets.

soul smart tip:

You will see the term "evidential medium" used in this book. An evidential medium is simply a mental medium (the medium uses his mind) who has developed the facility to receive and articulate details from the deceased. These can include personality; mannerisms; significant dates, places or objects; names or initials; and happy private memories. This evidence affirms that consciousness survives death.

And finally, please hold the emotions of love and joy in your heart when you use the Soul Smart techniques. The spirit world can be a fun-loving bunch and, believe me, your loved ones feel your laughter just as they do your sorrow, but laughter raises the vibration so much more. When you think of a fond shared memory, they know about it.

soul smart tip:

Feelings of love and joy help to harmonize your vibration with your beloved spirit people. Feelings of gratitude and brother- and sisterhood help to harmonize your vibration with your spirit guides and angels.

The dead and living communities both inform me that one day in the not-so-distant future we will have a communication device between our worlds. The technology for a sort of phone line between Heaven and Earth that will allow us to make calls to one another is being developed now on both sides of the veil. It will require a little more time to develop and fine-tune, but the spirit world assures us that it will be operative sooner than we might think.

Meanwhile, if you don't want to wait for 1-800-Dial-Heaven, it is time to turn to the next page of your own life!

CHAPTER TWO

one small medium

I OFTEN SAY THAT SPIRIT communication is like water. It follows the path of least resistance. Children are natural receivers of spirit communication because they are more open, and they are fresh from the spirit world. I'm going to share a little bit about my childhood to give you some perspective about what it is like to be a natural-born medium. Perhaps this will trigger you to remember an experience from your own childhood, or you might recognize that your child or grandchild is able to sense spirit, too!

A PECULIAR CHILD

"Get up, Susie! You're going to be late!" My mother's voice echoed down the hallway from the kitchen, pre-dawn on a school day. I had just started first grade. As usual, I did not want to get up because I was having too much fun.

I was out of my body and loving it! How much fun it is to fly! I was often out of my body at night, flying over mountaintops, rivers, and valleys. And this time, I wasn't flying alone. A red-haired boy held my hand. Together we soared through the air like superheroes. The boy never once spoke to me.

"Susie! Get. Up. Now."

My mother's voice sounded more than a little exasperated. Party pooper!

I began hearing familiar music in my mind. I heard this music when it was time to get back inside my body. It seemed to help me with that process. I wouldn't hear that otherworldly music again until a near-death experience that I had decades later.

Paranormal experiences were everyday occurrences in my childhood. Although I was an excellent student, school was the last place I wanted to be. I was an outsider at school, but very popular with the spirit world. They were my real friends!
I was bullied in first grade, and gosh, don't you detest bullying? It started because I couldn't seem to keep my mouth shut about the awesome things I saw that nobody else saw. I would get excited about seeing auras and spirit people, so I would talk about it. Sometimes I frightened the other children and some of the teachers. Forty years ago there were no TV programs or talk shows featuring psychic children or mediums, so I was called "Crazy Susie" and pushed around by children on the playground numerous times.

Sometime what seems, at the time, to be the worst that could happen becomes a blessing in disguise. That was true of my being bullied. Eventually, my grandfather, who was my father figure, asked me why I wanted to stay home from school, so I confided in him that I was being bullied and I told him why. I told him I often saw colorful lights and spirit people around the other children. To my amazement, Granddad believed me!

And it got better. My grandfather then said, "I can see them, too." My grandfather was an ordained Protestant minister who held doctorate degrees in religion and metaphysical science. He was a man of substance and character, and his understanding of the spirit world was well ahead of his time.

For the next few years, I would stay overnight at my grandparents' house on Fridays. We stayed up late and had long talks, and we found differences as we compared our abilities. He saw lights around people, but usually this happened only when they were about to die, whereas I saw them regularly and randomly. Like me, he traveled out of body starting in childhood.

On Saturdays, he would spend the afternoon in his private study to prepare his sermon for Sunday morning's church service, and sometimes nothing would come to him for hours. Then his study would fill with a bright, white light and the sermon flowed through him, sometimes so fast that he could barely write it all down. When I watched him preach from the pulpit, there was always white light all around him. During the sermons that were really on fire with passion, a large white funnel-shaped light appeared over my grandfather's head and extended several feet straight up in the air. Looking back, I now realize that my grandfather was communicating with the highest vibrational beings. Today I refer to them as "The Unity." More about that a bit later on!

My grandfather was also a hypnotherapist. Curious about his own past incarnations, he underwent a past life regression that was tape-recorded. While under hypnosis, surprisingly, my grandfather spoke in an unrecognizable language. The tape recording was reviewed by a university expert, who identified the language that my grandfather had been speaking under hypnosis as an ancient Inuit (Eskimo) dialect. But my grandfather had been born and raised in the United States and the only languages beyond English he had studied were Spanish and Latin. Today I think of him every time I conduct a past life regression for a client.

Did you have a grandparent whose words have stuck with you through life? My grandfather certainly had lots of sayings! Here is my favorite: "We live so far below our privileges as children of God." He said that everyone, and even the "least of these," is gifted in a unique way. We are put on the Earth to use our gifts, to be of service, and to bring Heaven to Earth.

A CHILD OF DEATH

As a child, I was often around death and dying. And I loved it! I accompanied my grandfather on his regular visits to hospitals and nursing homes, the places where most people died back then since there were no hospices. Some of the elderly who were dying would tell us they were being visited by loved ones in spirit. Today, these experiences are known as deathbed visitations. I remember seeing a blinking light over a woman's head as she lay in her nursing home bed; she died later that night. Many of the people we visited were lonely, especially those in nursing homes. Seeing the preacher's little granddaughter was the highlight of their week! Sometimes they reached out to me and squeezed my hand, and I felt their love and returned it with mine.

And when parishioners from our church died, my grandfather presided over their funerals. Guess who went with him? Me! That was when I learned that the people in spirit will nearly always show up at their funerals. Wouldn't you want to check in on your last Earthly party?

There was a young man from our church who had been killed as a soldier in the Vietnam War. His body was badly damaged so his coffin was kept closed. Having overheard a church parishioner say that the young man had been "blown into hamburger" by a grenade or land mine, I was relieved to see him in spirit at his funeral. He looked absolutely perfect, and he was carrying a tennis racket. When I later told his younger sister about seeing her brother in spirit, she was very happy. Her parents had allowed her to choose items to be placed in her brother's coffin, and one of the items she chose was his favorite tennis racket.

One day during our nursing home rounds my grandfather was in the room of a very sick man and ministering to him. This time, I was told to wait outside. I sat on a hallway bench where the nurses, who all knew me from previous visits, could keep watch over me. Looking back, they must have been curious as to why a young child would be content to hang out in a nursing home.

So I was coloring in a coloring book, probably outside the lines, when the most amazing, scary, and beautiful event occurred. The closed door to the dying man's room began to light up as if a spotlight were shining on the entire door. And then the man in spirit walked straight through the closed door! He was wearing pajamas. His feet were bare and slightly above the floor. He paused for a second, and then it was as though he recognized someone down the hall. He smiled, turned to the right, and began walking down the hall until he faded away. I gathered up the coloring books and crayons and stacked them neatly on the bench, and I donned my coat and gloves and stood there, waiting for my grandfather. *The man had gone to Heaven, so it must be time for us to go home.*

A moment later, the door opened, and my grandfather stood in the doorway. When he caught sight of me, all packed up and dressed to go home, he smiled and said, "You know, don't you." It was more a statement than a question.

Looking back, I am grateful to have learned at a young age that death is not the end. Death is a homecoming.

CHAPTER THREE

wake-up call

WHEN I WAS FOURTEEN years old I had a premonition that my beloved grandfather was going to die. There was no reason for me to be thinking this, since he was only fifty-six years old, trim, and in good health. Or so we thought. Because most of the predictions that I shared with family and close friends had come to fruition, my mother panicked when I told her I thought my grandfather was about to die. He was her father, and she cherished him. I wanted to see him, but we had moved to a town located two hours' drive away and I didn't yet drive.

My mother called my grandfather on the phone. I told him about my vision that he was about to die. He assured me that he wasn't going to die anytime soon. But I couldn't sleep. A few nights later, as I laid in bed, my grandfather opened my bedroom door and walked into the room. I sprang from my bed and into his arms.

He was smiling. We began to dance the box step, just as we had done at his Rotary Club's father-daughter dances every year. That's when he said, *"God has called me home,"* and I realized I was dancing with my beloved grandfather's spirit. We stood still now, and I could feel his hands on my shoulders as if to steady me. He told me that everything would be all right. He said to have faith and trust. And then he was gone.

I turned on the light and sank onto the bed, sobbing. A moment later, the phone rang and my mother received the news of her father's unexpected death at age fifty-six of sudden congestive heart failure.

soul smart tip:

Sometimes loved ones who have newly arrived in spirit will appear to you, in a dream while you are asleep or in a thought while you are awake, just to let you know that they're okay.

MEDIUM IN THE CLOSET

I was a teen medium who missed my grandfather and had nobody who could share my weird life. Occasionally I would find other teens who were interested in the paranormal, but all they wanted to do was tell ghost stories. My whole life was one big ghost story! I found myself unable to relate to other teens.

After high school graduation, I spent my young adulthood working full-time and going to college. I wanted to fit in! And that meant having a traditional career. I kept it secret from nearly everyone that in my spare time I was attending psychic development seminars, studying metaphysical books, and receiving mentoring on my mediumship abilities from teacher-mediums.

Why did I keep my hobby a secret? I was embarrassed. I thought it was cheesy to be a psychic medium and, frankly, it still is looked down on by some. I wanted to be taken seriously, so I worked very hard for my education and planned for a left-brain focused career! I earned a Bachelor's degree in Management, a Master's degree in Public Administration with a concentration in public affairs policy, and professional certifications.

Eventually, I was an administrative manager at one of the world's leading teaching and research institutions in California, and I became a founding administrative director at a center for leadership based at a Florida university. Over time, I became consumed with giving myself all the standard luxuries of life, and even many more things that I didn't need. Developing my mediumship abilities was a part-time hobby. Not only did I *not* use my gift of mediumship to help others then, but I *did* try to use it to win the lottery, which is a decidedly un-spiritual thing to do! But of course, I promised God that if He would let me win the lottery I would give half the money to charity. Needless to say, this did not work out well.

By my thirties, I was attending many more psychic and mediumship development workshops and group demonstrations. And at a weekend seminar twenty years ago in Miami, Florida, I did my first evidential mediumship reading as an adult for a total stranger. Our teacher for the seminar, James Van Praagh, is in these days a very well-known medium and spiritual teacher. I have since studied in group sessions with James several times.

During one of the exercises in James's workshop, we split

into pairs. The idea was to work with someone we knew nothing about. We first used psychometry to tune in to the person's energy. Psychometry is reading the residual energy that the person has left on an object that they alone have worn for some time; psychometry is not mediumship. Rather, psychometry is psychic work, meaning that one reads the energy that a person has left on an object.

I was paired with a man in his mid-forties. The man held my watch and proceeded to tell me that he saw a wedding with me. This was correct, as I had attended the wedding of a friend one day earlier. But when the man gave me my watch back and then tried to pick up on my loved ones, nothing happened.

It was my turn to do psychometry. I held the man's watch, and immediately I began seeing pictures in my mind of the man when he was a little boy. Before I could describe these images, the most amazing thing happened. Directly behind the man, I saw a large white door appear. The door opened, and in walked a much older man in spirit! I heard the word "father," and then the words "heart attack" in my mind. Then the man pointed at the watch that I held in my hand for the psychometry exercise and I heard the word, "mine."

I was worried that I would get this wrong, but I mustered my courage and blurted quickly, "There is a man standing behind you. He looks a lot like you except he has no hair on top of his head, just hair on the sides. He says he is your father. He had a heart attack."

Then I held up the man's watch in my hand and said, "Your father says this was his watch. I think he's happy that you wear it now." Everything I received was one hundred percent correct, and I don't know who was more surprised at the accuracy of the information!

After that experience, I began to meet with friends to practice meditation and tuning in to the spirit world. All of this was done in secret since I had no plans to come out as a medium. My priority was to have a successful career as a respected professional, and to buy lots of things.

WAKING UP TO MY CALLING

One day ten years ago, it became clear to my spirit guides that I was not fulfilling my life's purpose, so I experienced what I think of as my wake-up call. I had left my job as a director in a university a few years before to help my husband in our business. After that, I left the family business for a good job offer as a manager in human resources for a multi-billion-dollar company. I was also enrolled in a weekend Ph.D. program in human resources development. While my professional life was going great, my physical health was terrible: I was plagued by sinus infections and respiratory problems. I decided to consult an allergy specialist.

This is where my wake-up call happened, right in that doctor's office. I had a near-death experience during, of all things, the boring process of allergy-testing. During a scratch-test, a technician places tiny amounts of allergens (the things that you might be allergic to) under the skin of your arm. These allergy tests are perfectly safe, except in very rare circumstances in which a severe allergic reaction occurs. So my testing began, and what happened next was both terrifying and awesome. It forever changed my mind.

While the technician was injecting allergens under the skin of my arm, I began feeling nauseated and a little too warm for comfort.

When I mentioned this, the technician agreed that the room was a bit stuffy. She adjusted the air conditioning accordingly. "My throat hurts," I said. The technician looked at me. Later I would learn that my sun-tanned face had turned ghostly white. She blurted, "I'm getting a doctor!" I was alone for a few seconds as I began to feel as though I was underwater, gasping for air. Then I heard footsteps running in the hallway, and two doctors and two technicians entered the room. The technicians held me in an upright position, one at each of my shoulders, as I sat on the exam table. One doctor asked me how I was feeling, while the other doctor was pulling supplies out of the medical cabinet and flinging them onto the counter.

"My throat . . . Help . . . me . . ."

NEAR-DEATH EXPERIENCE

I managed to get the words out between gasps. Then the strangest sound was coming from my throat: it was a honking noise, like that of a goose. I stopped breathing. My heart rate slowed. I heard one of the doctors say, "Keep holding her up!"

I knew, I was standing about two feet behind my body and about six inches above the floor. I then realized that I felt wonderful! And that is when I heard beautiful music. It was the same music I had heard as a child during those out-of-body experiences. The music was lush and inviting, washing over me in waves.

The scene in front of me, with the medical staff and my body, seemed surreal. I felt disconnected from all of that; I had become the observer. I saw my body slumped over even though two technicians, one on each side of me, were holding it up. My chin lay on my chest.

I had the odd thought that the back of my hair needed combing, but that faded quickly as I stopped caring about my body altogether.

It became even weirder. The medical people who were working on my body didn't even look real anymore: they were shiny and one-dimensional, and their eyes were dull and dead-looking. Then I realized that they all were moving in slow motion! One of the doctors was prepping a hypodermic needle in slow motion while the other was punching numbers into a phone, also in slow motion. Later I would learn that he was calling an ambulance.

Then I sensed a presence standing behind me. This presence reached out and wrapped loving arms around me, melting my fear away. Something seemed familiar about the presence. I detected a hint of a fragrance. It was my beloved dead grandfather's cologne. My grandfather had his arms around me! I said to him, "Granddad! I've missed you so much!" I felt cherished and protected, a contented feeling that was far beyond what words can describe.

My grandfather said nothing. He continued to stand behind me with his arms around my shoulders. He held me tightly. I had a feeling that if my grandfather weren't holding me, I might float away. Beautiful colors swirled around us, and they undulated as if they were living beings. The Heavenly music continued. I had a strong urge to follow the music, to find the source.

That is when I heard an unfamiliar voice that sounded robotic and tinny say, "Your work hasn't started." I felt an intense rush of pressure on the top of my head, and I was vacuum-sucked out of my grandfather's arms. I was being pushed and pulled back into my physical body; I had no choice in the matter.

The doctor had injected my body with something to stop the

anaphylaxis. Next, the medical technicians laid my body down on the exam table. One second I was looking at my body, and the next second I was pushed-pulled back into it. I heard the doctor say, "Is she breathing?" And then I gasped for air.

I was back in my body. My throat was on fire and my chest felt as if an elephant were sitting on it. I had managed just a few ragged breaths when the paramedics burst into the room. One of the paramedics rushed towards me with what I recognized from television shows was a heart defibrillator. Thankfully, it turned out to be unnecessary. An oxygen mask was put on me. The next thing I knew, I was lying on a gurney that was being placed into an ambulance.

In the ambulance, my emotions ran rapidly, and I felt confused. The paramedic was very reassuring. He told me how fortunate I was to have anaphylaxis in a doctor's office, where my life could be saved.

"You should buy a lottery ticket," the paramedic said with a kindly pat on my shoulder. Little did he know the irony of his comment! For years I had tried to win the lottery using my abilities, but no more. That no longer mattered. In fact, I had won something of even greater value. I had felt the peace that surpasses all understanding.

I SEE DEAD PEOPLE EVERYWHERE

After the hospital, the doctor advised me to rest for a day or two. I was fine, but my body and my emotions had been through a shock. I ignored the doctor's advice. I couldn't wait to see everyone at work.

I wanted to hug everyone! I was exuberant with joy. At the time, I was working in a very responsible human resources management position at the corporate headquarters of a multi-billion-dollar company. But I didn't want to act like a buttoned-up corporate clone any longer. I wanted to tell people that "it's all about love."

At work, a colleague approached me. He told me that he, too, had experienced a near-death episode. He had flat-lined as a child with complications from pneumonia, and all he could remember of nearly dying was seeing a white light, a bunch of people smiling in the light, and that was it. He was curious to hear about my near-death experience, while nobody else at work even cared.

When I confided in my friend that I had the ability to speak with the dead, I held my breath in anticipation of his derisive laughter. Instead, he asked me a question that I would hear thousands of times over the ensuing years: "Who do you see around me?"

I took a deep breath. Spirits were lining up, and I began describing them to him, one by one. He was taking notes at a furious pace and giving me almost no feedback. Some of the spirits showed me their faces. Others held objects of significance in their hands. I was completely in the flow of the reading. Then about halfway through, I became aware of a separate group of spirits in the room. They were helping the spirits to communicate with me. I noted that the spirit guide with the red hair looked very familiar to me.

When I finished, I searched my colleague's face for his reaction. He seemed to be overwhelmed with emotion. It forever changed my mind. Much of it was highly personal and not knowable unless I was indeed connecting with his loved ones in Heaven. "Wow. I don't think you are going to be working here much longer," he mused. "Did you ever stop to think: maybe this was your wake-up call?"

That was when I remembered the voice I had heard in the doctor's office that day, that had said, "Your work hasn't started."

soul smart tip:

As John Lennon said, "Life is what happens to you while you are busy making other plans." The Universe will call your attention to what is important in your life. Pay attention to what is getting your attention.

After I gave that amazing reading to the executive at work, I felt good: cocky, really. But that good feeling did not last long.

Within days, I was sick with a severe sinus infection. This was not the first time: I had been getting antibiotic-resistant sinus infections, one after another, and lately they were progressing into pneumonia; plus, I was working too hard. My job was demanding, I was enrolled in a weekend Ph.D. program, and I was going to medium development seminars besides. The pace was too much! I had become overwhelmed, sick, and very tired.

I fell into a depression. My mind replayed that day in the doctor's office when I had suffered the anaphylaxis. *Why didn't I die? Why didn't Heaven want me?* I began to think of myself as "Heaven's Reject." I could not figure out my life's purpose. Even more troubling, thanks to the dead, I never could find a moment of peace. They now followed me nearly everywhere! Apparently a near-death experience can heighten sensitivities. For me, that meant the constant uninvited presence of spirits who were complete strangers to me.

Dead people stood by my bed nightly while I tried to sleep.

Dead people sat at my kitchen counter watching me cook dinner.

A dead woman handed me a towel as I got out of the shower.

A dead person knocked on the door to the toilet. And no one was at home but me!

My solution was to start drinking. Heavily. I had wine every night for a while, and then one glass turned into two. I was well on my way to becoming an alcoholic. Overwhelmed, depressed, and self-medicated.

One day I found the website for the International Association for Near-Death Studies (iands.org). I was supposed to be writing a paper for my Ph.D. program. Instead, I spent that entire Sunday speed-reading everything on the IANDS website. Afterwards, I felt a sense of relief. I wasn't the only person whose life was changed following a near-death experience! I didn't feel the need to reach for a bottle of wine that night and seldom ever again.

After reading about other people's near-death experiences, I began to understand what had happened to me. My brief brush with mortality had flipped the "medium switch" to full-power! In my usual analytical way, I reasoned that if my mediumship could be turned "on," then it could also be turned "off." I just needed to find a way to make that happen. I attended every workshop, seminar, and book-signing I could find that featured mediums and people who knew about near-death, whether they were experiencers or researchers. Most attendees were trying to learn how to better tune in. But I needed to learn how to tune out!

Meanwhile, I had sinus surgery in an effort to alleviate my frequent sinus infections. The sinus surgery went well. Unfortunately, I contracted a staph infection in the hospital. Now I was battling something serious: invasive MRSA (methicillin-resistant Staphylococcus aureus). MRSA is a form of bacterial infection that is resistant to numerous antibiotics. Invasive MRSA kills the tissue of the skin and internal organs. I had horrible open sores on my body that felt like cigar burns. The only known cure was weeks of infusion treatments with very strong drugs given to me intravenously in a chemotherapy-type of setting. For the next several weeks I battled sepsis (blood poisoning), osteomyelitis (bone infection), and fibromyalgia (widespread musculoskeletal pain).

Being deathly ill actually turned out to be yet another blessing in disguise! I meditated for hours every day. I learned how to truly sit in the power and feel my spirit's oneness with the Source. I reread all my books on mediumship and psychic development. I felt the presence of spirit in and around me. And my illness helped me to stumble upon an ability to project my consciousness completely out of my body at will. One day while I was simply resting after an infusion treatment, my consciousness spontaneously sprang out of my body and hovered near the ceiling. And, guess what? I felt no pain! I could see that I was tethered to my body by a thin strand of whitish-gold light. I felt great! And I began to do this once or twice a day. It was a respite from the physical pain in my body, since my body was so ill while my consciousness remained perfect. But that was not the only benefit I received from being ill!

In mediumship, part of the consciousness of the medium leaves the body in order to connect with the consciousness of the spirits. Some mediums spend years developing their power centers to be able to go out-of-body. I was doing it spontaneously. Out of the body, and loving it!

MY SPIRIT GUIDE

One day during my infusion treatment I felt particularly ill. Chills wracked my body so hard that my teeth chattered. I couldn't wait to get home and enter my semi-conscious state so I could leave my body, if only for a few minutes. My nurse drove me home and helped me to the sofa. She covered me with several blankets, then placed the candle on the table and lit it, exactly as I had requested.

The moment the nurse left me alone, I lost control. First, I cursed God. Then I pleaded with Him for help. I was sick and tired of being sick and tired! It was harder to meditate that day, but eventually I did meditate and leave my body. That's when something very unexpected happened.

As I floated near the ceiling, this time I became aware of several spirit people floating with me. One of the spirit people looked familiar. It was the red-haired little boy! Except now, he appeared to be about thirty-five years old. He had red hair, a mustache, and a neatly trimmed beard. His eyes were filled with compassion.

"Who are you?" I asked.

The spirit man said, "Your guide." I did not see his lips move, but I did hear his voice in my mind.

And then something dawned on me. "You're the boy who walked me to school!" I told him that I remembered flying with him and astral-traveling when I was a child. I also recognized him from the day I did the reading for my work colleague; he had been a helper to the dead who spoke with me.

The spirit guide smiled, but I was now feeling a wave of self-righteous indignation.

"Can't you see I'm sick?"

My guide continued to smile. He said, "You are healing."

"Well, where have you been all this time?" I implored my spirit guide, thinking that he had left me when I was a child.

"What do you mean?" He continued to smile benevolently. Then his expression became more serious, with a new intensity in his violet-blue eyes. He said, "I have never left you. I will never leave you."

In that instant I felt so intensely cherished and protected, I thought for a moment that my heart might explode. This spirit man was my master spirit guide! From that day on, I would see him every day without exception. I felt that he was a part of my soul.

WHEN THE STUDENT IS READY, THE TEACHER APPEARS

Five months later I had a reading with an exceptional evidential medium. His name was Alan Arcieri, and he would become an important teacher for me. Although Alan transitioned to the spirit world a year after we met, he continued to help me in spirit form, especially during my early years of being a professional medium.

When I first came to Alan for a reading, he had just my first name. And I was a terrible sitter, because I gave him no feedback. I barely said a word; I think I was just too nervous. Today, that drives me nuts when the sitter won't even say "yes" or "no" because so much more opens up when we acknowledge our messages. I had never had a private reading before, and the energy around Alan felt amazing.

Alan immediately picked up on my master spirit guide, whose name I would later learn was LeoRoy. Alan explained to me that in a past life, LeoRoy was incarnated on Earth while I was LeoRoy's spirit guide in training. Here I would like to point out that several years later a second medium gave exactly the same validation to me, even though I had never mentioned that detail. With no prompting from me and no knowledge of my recent circumstances, Alan mentioned the physical suffering I had recently experienced from illness. He explained that the illness was an integral part of the preparation for my greater work. The spirit world was pushing me into being a medium and a spiritual teacher and I was behind on my timeline, the life plans that I, and my team, had developed before I was born. I was absolutely a medium and if I were to continue to deny it, I would suffer even more. There was no way Alan could have known my secret! But, of course, the spirit world knew.

Alan also brought in my grandfather in spirit, correctly calling him "a man of the cloth with the highest vibrational energy." My grandfather told me to lean on him, and he would help me. Immediately after that reading, I became Alan's avid student. Looking back, I can't believe how patiently and thoroughly he answered all my questions! It was a productive and exciting year of learning the many facets of communicating with people who were no longer in bodies.

Eventually, I was ready to do practice readings for sitters.

A friend arranged these readings for me and, on my instruction, she provided only each sitter's first name. Often I was as surprised as my sitters by the accuracy of the information I received from their beloved people in spirit. My friends and I were sitting in a mediumship development circle, too, and Alan provided ideas for practice exercises. I felt my abilities becoming stronger by the day. Thanks to Alan, I learned to build my personal power and maintain my center, grounding, and protection. I regained my inner peace. The spirits couldn't bother me anymore, unless I invited them in.

THE REALITY OF MONEY AND MEDIUMSHIP

At first, I could do only one or two readings a week because I had a demanding full-time career. This was frustrating since I knew that I could help more people if I could do mediumship full time. But how could I pay all our bills with fees from readings? This is a dilemma faced by many mediums, worldwide.

In fact, many good mediums must work a second job to pay their bills, which means they can't help many people at all. Please don't begrudge a professional medium the right to charge the fee he sets! Unless the medium has someone supporting him, or he has inherited money, he must pay all his bills from his earnings as a medium. Think about your own monthly bills! There is the mortgage/ rent plus insurances, groceries, taxes, car payments, gas, medical, and so on. And it's not as if mediums can do readings forty hours a week; that would be impossible, as I explained earlier. Being on TV doesn't make us rich either, so please understand that we've got to charge for our services.

Then, of course, when word gets out about the quality of a medium's readings, the demand grows and there are dozens of phone calls and emails going back and forth daily with clients. The medium then needs to hire an appointment booker, a webmaster, maybe a graphic artist . . . and guess where the money to pay them all must come from? As I tell my medium students, "God doesn't write paychecks." It amazes me how many people who could easily afford to buy a reading will expect a free reading or a discount. A few years ago I gave a free reading to a woman who said she "couldn't afford" to pay me. She had a wonderful reading, and afterward she joined my Facebook page and posted a "thank you" note. Then a week later she posted more pictures from the luxury Alaska cruise that she was currently taking. And this was someone who couldn't afford to pay for her reading? You will find that there are good mediums available at all price points. Ask a friend for a referral. Or attend a service at a local spiritualist church, and ask about events where there are free or low-cost readings.

These fiscal realities, combined with my decision to quit my job and become a full-time medium, ultimately caused my husband and me to sell everything and altogether change our lifestyle. We moved to an area where we could live on much less. We live comfortably, but not lavishly. And I have the privilege of witnessing every day the healing power of connecting with spirit! I have a loving husband of thirty years, two adorable dogs, and a happy home that is filled with gratitude.

WHAT IS MEDIUMSHIP?

I am a mental medium who practices evidential mediumship. Most of the public is familiar with the terms "psychic medium" or "spiritual medium," and, while those terms are generally correct for mediums who work as I do, they are quite imprecise. To put it into perspective, calling me a medium is like calling your dentist, optometrist, and podiatrist all "doctor." You are not wrong about that, but there are different kinds of doctors!

I am an *evidential medium*. As I mentioned earlier, this means that I am a mental medium who has developed the facility to receive and articulate details from the deceased. The details provide the evidence that consciousness never dies.

soul smart tip:

An evidential mental medium reading is a triadic communication, meaning the energies of the deceased, the medium, and the sitter each play a role in the reading's level of success. It is the spirit that completely controls what evidence will be given, and it is the medium's job to relay that evidence in the clearest possible detail. The sitter is responsible to release expectations about what the deceased "should" say and allow the reading to unfold naturally without trying to control it.

Have you heard it said that "all mediums are psychic, but not all psychics are mediums?" Here is what this means. A psychic connects to the sitter's aura and reads the sitter's aura, which contains the sitter's past, present information and also some future potentialities. A medium can do that, but when a medium is conducting a genuine mediumship reading he isn't reading the sitter's aura; instead, he is connecting directly to the spirit person's consciousness and receiving the information from there. The term "psychic medium" is redundant because all mediums are psychic. But as you have just heard, not all psychics are mediums.

There are several types of mediumship: mental, physical, trance, and healing mediumship. Mediumship goes back hundreds of years and has a rich history that includes many fascinating people. For more information on the subject of mediums and their history, I highly recommend that you read *A Lawyer Presents the Evidence for the Afterlife* by Victor and Wendy Zammit. It is required reading for my mediumship mentoring students.

Now it's time to talk about the elephant in the room. Death. What happens when you die? Here is the answer.

— CHAPTER FOUR —

what to expect when you die

DYING IS EASY; IT is living after injury or illness that can be unpleasant. While you're alive, you have an energy cord that connects your soul to your physical body. When you die, this energy cord will be severed and you will be disconnected permanently from your body. There is no going back. This is different from a near-death experience. The energy cord remains intact during a near-death experience; otherwise you wouldn't be able to re-enter your body.

One or more loved ones, usually beloved spirit people or pets, will be there to help with your next step. A loved one will extend a hand or motion to you. This is your invitation to merge with the light and travel to your Heavenly home. Please don't hesitate for a second!

Go quickly. Once your energy cord has been severed, you will be at risk of becoming Earthbound (a ghost) unless you let go of your own free will and enter into the light. Your loved ones will invite you, but they cannot force you. Remember, you can visit with your living loved ones later, so don't dawdle at death. Get thee into the light. Quickly!

soul smart tip:

The spirit world tells us that we can ask for whomever we want to be the first to greet us when we die. All you'll need to do is say your chosen person's or pet's first name, and ask that particular loved one to be there first when you die. The loved one of your choice will hear you, and will be there at exactly the moment of death, if not a bit earlier.

I would like to clarify that you are not required to summon a loved one in spirit to meet you at death. Although it's a nice option! Just before your death comes, the spirit world will get word, and the right loved one will come to help you.

NEXT STOP: HALL OF HEALING

You will probably make a pit stop at a Hall of Healing. You won't want to miss this opportunity. The Halls of Healing are sort of like fancy spas that have been attuned to a high, healing vibration. Here you will find that a room has been prepared for you. Now you can take a nap to recharge. This helps to ensure that your transition goes smoothly. Don't worry about missing your funeral because someone will awaken you on time. Nearly everyone does attend his own funeral. If you wish to rest more after your funeral, you can return to the Hall of Healing and rest some more, and awaken whenever you are ready. This is never a permanent state. Upon awakening, you will hear and feel every kind thought and prayer that a loved one on Earth has said for you.

DETOUR: SPIRIT REHABILITATION

There is a specialized place designed to help someone who dies in a state of complete exhaustion, perhaps due to a protracted illness. Special help might also be needed if, just before death, a person was in a state of extreme emotional upset due to suicide or a sudden, shocking death, as in a vehicle accident. This place is affectionately nicknamed "Spirit Rehab," and it is located within the Halls of Healing.

In Spirit Rehab, one is surrounded by love and compassion from healing angels and guides. If one is in denial about being dead, the healing angels and guides will be dressed as doctors and nurses. This could take a few months in Earth time, but there will be a period of alertness so that one can attend one's own funeral. Waking up to one's new reality is a bit slower in Spirit Rehab. It's like coming out of heavy anesthesia. This is not a permanent state, of course; nothing ever is. One awakens when one is rested and ready. Upon awakening, one hears every kind thought and prayer that a loved one on Earth has said.

Several spirits have said that some of the rooms in Spirit

Rehab are named after saints. Most frequently mentioned to me are the Saint Francis Room and the Saint Germain room, although we have not received much detail about the differences between these healing rooms.

Those who commit suicide generally spend the most time resting in Spirit Rehab. This is why it usually takes longer after death to get a sign from a loved one who has killed himself. It also explains any delay for that loved one to get ready to communicate clearly with you through a medium. Suicides need extra time in Spirit Rehab, and when they first wake up they will be a bit foggy for Earth-time days or weeks. This temporary fogginess will fade. Be patient!

After resting in Spirit Rehab, suicides must do whatever it takes in order to forgive themselves. This usually means going to classes, receiving counseling, or participating in other healing modalities. All this is designed to help them forgive themselves for making the ultimate mistake of ending their precious lives. Even though nobody in the spirit world judges or in any way looks down on them, I haven't met anyone yet who said they would ever commit suicide again.

Suicide is never part of anyone's life plan. I politely beg to differ with those who say that it is. A person who commits suicide may have had an exit point in their life plan around that time, but it wouldn't be a suicide because I have yet to hear from anyone in the spirit world that suicide is part of a soul's plan.

Because I have done so many readings for bereaved parents, I have heard parents say they thought of killing themselves to be with their child in Heaven. That would be a mistake! Think long and hard. Your spirit loved ones are over there, bragging about how wonderful you are! They are proud of you. Even though they miss being with you, their greatest hope is that you will get the most out of each day of your life. If you kill yourself to be with a loved one, you will be very disappointed because you won't be with them for a long time. You'll be in Spirit Rehab, resting and probably kicking yourself in the arse for having given up so easily! Never kill yourself. Stay here and see your life through until the final day. I promise that later on you will understand the reasons for your suffering and what you really have accomplished! You won't fully comprehend all of it until later, so stop trying to figure out now why things happen.

soul smart tip:

No matter what state you are in when you arrive in the spirit world, there is a place where you can rest and recharge your spiritual batteries. And then you can resume your wonderful life between lives!

HALLS OF REUNION

After you have enjoyed exactly the amount of healing rest you need, your aura will transport you to a Hall of Reunion. These Halls of Reunion are popular places! Each of them includes lots of rooms, including rooms for welcome-home parties where new arrivals are reunited with their beloved spirit people and pets. When you arrive after death, you will realize that you accomplished more than you thought you did, and you will be welcomed home with a party! The spirit community may also hold a parade in your honor. All this fanfare won't be because you were famous or filthy rich, but because you mostly did your best. It may surprise you to learn that your most celebrated accomplishments will be your acts of compassion and service. Everyone can see in your aura all the compassion and forgiveness you gave others and yourself while you were on Earth.

There are Life Review rooms and Orientation rooms in the Halls of Reunion as well. The Life Review rooms are exactly what you might think. Here, you will review all of your life's thoughts, words, actions, and failures to act. You will feel exactly how you made others feel. You will see clearly where you met your goals and where you came up short. If you mostly did the best that you could on Earth, you will know it. Nobody judges you but you! The review is intended to help you realize all that you have accomplished and to help you grow.

Orientation rooms are where you meet with your spiritual team. Your team members are your spirit guides, angels, and loved ones from your soul group. Here, you will begin remembering who you truly are as a soul. You may have several meetings in the Orientation rooms. Most souls have one quick meeting first, and then head off to their welcome-home party!

soul smart tip:

Almost everyone chooses to attend his own funeral or memorial service. And almost everyone attends his welcome party, where all his beloved spirit people and pets gather to say, "Welcome Home."

WHERE WE LIVE AFTER DEATH

Your aura will automatically transport you to the Heavenly realm where you will live. The aura is the electromagnetic energy field that surrounds you. Your aura is sort of an ethereal database, and stored within it are the energies of all your thoughts, words, and actions on Earth. Unconditional love, compassion, and forgiveness carry the highest vibrational energies. When you have these high vibrational energies in your aura, it will transport you to a beautiful realm where positive souls like you reside. You will have a period of orientation and a welcome-home party. All your beloved spirit people and pets will be there, and ancestors who died before you were born will happily introduce themselves. It is an ecstatically joyous time.

soul smart tip:

There is no judgment by anyone else, but we do evaluate ourselves. After death, you will have a 360 degree life review, where you will feel the impacts of your thoughts, words, and actions on Earth. It is wise to work on being as positive as possible while you are still alive. Monitor your thoughts and keep them as loving as humanly possible. Be kind to people and animals and help them however you can.

WHAT HAPPENS WHEN A PET DIES

Pets, being purely souls of love, don't need a life review, healing, or orientation. They are immediately young, healthy, and whole, no matter how old or how sick they were at death. I want you to know that every pet that has connected with me during a reading has been perfectly happy and whole. And when they come through with the words "Thank you," I know they are saying, "Thank you for letting me go." The gift of having our pet professionally euthanized when it's time is the greatest gift of unconditional love that we can give, especially when we are there with them through the process.

Pets like to be playful, so when you think of your dog, cat, horse, bird, ferret, mouse, or other pet who has died, try to remember how they were when they were young and energetic. They have everything they need except for you, and they do miss you, but the good news is that, where they are now, time does not seem to matter. Even if decades pass before you join them, it will have seemed like only moments to your pet, who remembers your life together and loves you. Always.

IS THERE A HELL?

Years ago, a Baptist minister friend of mine observed, "Susanne, this is hell right now. We're all just helping each other until we can go home to Heaven."

When we talk about the Lower Realms—or hell, if you prefer—obviously we are not talking about you! But most of us are curious: what really happens after death to those who are evil on the Earth? Here I'm referring to violence and the infliction of pain upon others; acts which come from and foster the lowest vibrational energies. I haven't heard many of the dead use the word "hell." The spirit people generally use the terms the "Lowers" or "The Outer

Darkness" or "Darkness" in referring to the lowest realms.

While there seems to be no individual Satan, there are different types of beings that inhabit The Lowers. One that I have heard about is called a "Collector." Collectors are low-vibrational beings that typically attach their energies to the dregs of humankind such as murderers, molesters, animal abusers, and people like that. Collectors attach to evil human beings to feed on their negative energies. Later, when the evil human finally dies from whatever cause, the Collector will escort him to the Lowers. This is a sadistic and unnecessary act, because the newly-dead person's negative aura would naturally transport him to a lower realm. But Collectors like to get their jollies, and they can't attach to decent people, so they wait for evil people to die and then make them think they are being "dragged to hell." It's ugly, but not completely hopeless, as you are about to hear.

EVEN THE LOWEST CAN GROW

"For you grow to Heaven, you don't go to Heaven. It is within thine own conscience that ye grow there."
—*Edgar Cayce*

My friends in the spirit world assure us that The Creator never deserts any soul. There are volunteer teams from higher realms who try to help those in the Lowers. These volunteers are accompanied by warrior angels of light to protect them from absorbing any negative energies.

The volunteer rescue groups look long and hard, praying to locate a soul, any soul, who is capable and ready to grow out of The Lowers. Even slightly higher realms allow these souls to convalesce and continue the tedious process of receiving and accepting forgiveness. They can work on the hard task of forgiving themselves. My healing and Reiki spirit guide, Wakana, is one of the most determined souls I know. She describes her visits to The Lowers as exhausting and seldom fruitful. Because the souls have free will, they cannot be forced to grow spiritually. We are told that those in the Lowers cannot even visit realms higher than the Earth without first growing spiritually.

Whew, that was heavy stuff! Quick now, think about funny cat videos on YouTube, and don't spend another minute thinking about lower realms. Heaven is your true home! Regular people who do their best will end up in a very nice place after death; a place that ancient Vikings referred to as the Summerland, where all is beautiful and serene. You'll arrive there when it is your time. Meanwhile, observe the Golden Rule and give people and animals the compassion and respect that you would like to receive from them.

—— CHAPTER FIVE ——

life between lives

WE LIVE ON EARTH while we are in our bodies. And then, when our bodies have died, we live on the "other side of life", a beautiful place also known as the spirit world or Heaven. But why don't we remember much about our life between lives? Well, think about it: If you knew exactly why you are here and what you came here to do, that would be like having the teacher give you the answers to the test questions. How would you be able to learn anything?

Many people in Heaven think of us almost as their children. We on Earth are like children who are away at summer camp. We are having adventures and mishaps, and sometimes we become homesick, and we yearn to contact our loved ones who are waiting patiently at home. And that is where spirit communication comes in.

soul smart tip:

While you are incarnate, which means living in your body, you can remember little or nothing about your life in the spirit world. Forgetting who you are as an eternal soul allows you to immerse yourself in the Earthly experiences that you need right now. And that, in turn, enables you to grow as a soul. This is why during past-life regression hypnosis, you will recall only the events from past lives, or from life in between lives, that you are ready to recall.

DEAD AND LOVING IT

To better understand how to communicate with your beloved spirit people, it helps to know a little more about what their world is like. In the spirit world, the concept of One Mind, the Universal Consciousness, is acknowledged. It seems that everyone knows there is no separation between souls, and no separation between us and the Source. Most souls in the spirit world don an individual, physical appearance. It's a clever conceit, this wearing of an individual appearance, and it makes sense. Looking like a person, a youthful and very attractive one, makes it so much easier to participate in activities. You can continue to learn, grow spiritually, and have lots of fun!

Because all the Universal Laws continue to apply, including free will, each soul has its own individual thoughts, words, and actions. Everyone looks amazingly beautiful. It's like those soap operas on TV where nobody seems to age! You might choose to look like your young self as you were on Earth, or you might look completely different; it's up to you what appearance you choose to wear. But when it's time to connect with your loved ones on Earth, you will always look like a perfect version of the "you" that they remember so they will know that it's really you!

Dying doesn't make anyone become spontaneously enlightened. It doesn't bring anyone to instant nirvana, although we do feel better being out of our bodies. I find this to be good news! Imagine how boring it would be if, after death, we became nothing but blissed-out airheads floating around mindlessly with no purpose. Thankfully, our life in Heaven between lifetimes on Earth is much more meaningful and joyful.

Many of the so-called dead are considerably livelier than the so-called living! That's because Heaven is a vibrant, active place where you are free to create your own bliss. This is accomplished through many means, including art, music, theater, sciences, architecture, teaching, gardening, sports, and many other forms of individual and group expression. Work is like play, because you can do what you most enjoy. Some of the spirits say they are busier now than when they were alive. And they are loving it! If you want to know more about the different realms and the continued growth of the soul after physical death, I recommend the book *Your Eternal Self* by R. Craig Hogan.

THE DEAD DON'T EXACTLY KNOW YOUR FUTURE

I wish I had a dollar for every time a client asked me for a prediction from a relative who is in spirit form. "Ask my grandma, when will I get married and have children?" News flash! Grandma cannot know what you are going to decide to do, since you have free will!

soul smart tip:

Dying doesn't make anyone all-knowing. The best your spirit loved ones and living psychics can do is to read the strong potentials of your opportunities and challenges, based on your current path. But you can change your path. You have free will!

Based upon my having conducted thousands of readings and countless conversations with master spirit guides, I have it on good authority that you can change your life in an instant. Your master life plan is malleable, because it's based on your thoughts, words, and actions. While I do believe that before you were born you planned to have certain life experiences, you have the precious gift of free will. At any point during your life on Earth you might opt on a soul level (your higher self) to delete an upcoming experience. Or your higher self might choose to take an early exit point or a later one. It can also decide to have a certain experience in a way that is different from what was originally charted.

DEATH IS A CHANGE OF ADDRESS

We have two hundred years of research from quantum physicists, researchers, and scientists proving that consciousness lives forever. Consciousness cannot be destroyed. And you are your consciousness! After your loved ones died, only their bodies were gone. Their memories, emotions, and love bonds are still intact and always will be.

"Energy cannot be created or destroyed. It can only be changed from one form to another."

—*Albert Einstein*

"All matter originates and exists only by virtue of a force . . . We must assume behind this force the existence of a conscious and intelligent Mind. This Mind is the matrix of all matter."

—*Max Planck*

soul smart tip:

Think of death as simply a change of address! Remember when you moved from one city to another? Perhaps you were happy or excited about your big move, but moving didn't transform your personality overnight. Death is simply the soul moving out of the body. You keep, fully intact, your personality, memories, and emotional bonds with your loved ones. After death, you will continue to be YOU. And you will have ample opportunities to learn and grow spiritually if you so choose.
There's that "free will" thing again.

SEX AFTER DEATH

I have it on good authority that sexual intercourse—yes, sex!—is possible in the spirit world and that anyone can do it. After all,

Heaven really is Heaven! But sex is different in the afterlife. It is even more sensational! Heavenly "bodies" are youthful, attractive, and resonating at a higher frequency than Earthly bodies. Even though, like Ken and Barbie dolls, we are not necessarily anatomically correct in Heaven, this is a blessing because soul energies blend perfectly and spectacularly every time.

Recently I had a conversation with a friend who is a grief educator. As I was telling Sandi about sex after death, she asked if my guides knew whether there was a product, like an energy, that is produced when two souls without bodies have intimate intercourse. I was still in my zone of doing readings and surrounded by my guides, so they quickly answered her question. Apparently everybody is interested in sex! (Who knew?) I was shown what the product of this intercourse between two discarnate beings looks like, and it was beautiful! I saw a bright blue sky, lush green grass, and then a beautiful flower with rainbow-colored petals sprang up. The flower was the product of the intercourse. The flower quickly grew several feet tall, and it swayed and made sounds similar to wind chimes.

SEX BETWEEN A LIVING PERSON AND A PARTNER IN SPIRIT

First, I want to be absolutely clear that this is consensual sex we are talking about. If the thought of having sex with a spirit frightens you, you can skip this entire section!

Over the years I have spoken with dozens of clients who believed they had had sexual intercourse with their partners, sometimes months or years after the partner died. Four clients allowed me to interview them, three women and one man. All four interviewees said the following:

1. They had been asleep and their spirit partner awakened them;

2. They gave some form of consent to their spirit partner such as a head nod or open arms;

3. They could feel the partner's body as though the spirit partner was incarnate, including touching their skin and feeling the weight of the body. Some described having goose bumps even though they felt warmth; and

4. They experienced climax, during the event, in their sleep.

In these four interviews, the earliest incident of lovemaking with the spirit partner happened approximately six months after death. The latest was nearly seven years after the partner's death. One interviewee said the incident happened only one time, while the other three said their lovemaking was ongoing, from one to three times per year.

DO THE DEAD GRIEVE?

Grief does exist within the spirit world, but it is a cherished feeling, not a painful one! It certainly is nowhere near as difficult as the grief we feel on Earth when our loved one transitions to Heavenly home. The dead would like you to know why the separation isn't as difficult for them, so here goes! On the Earth plane, separation has long been our way of life. We convince ourselves that we are apart from The Creator and apart from each other. Nothing could be further from the truth! All of us are connected, but we forget that when we are on Earth.

For the spirit world, grief is sacred. It is honored and savored. To the spirits, grieving the separation is a bittersweet reminder of the eternal love bond that they share with the living. Grief does not debilitate anyone in the spirit world. Yes, they miss us! Remember, they took their personalities and all their memories with them. But they can see us any time they wish, although of course our privacy is respected. Usually!

The spirit world has many discussion circles for those who miss their loved ones on Earth. In these discussion circles, the spirits gather to talk about news of the loved ones they have temporarily left behind. These are happy, not sad, gatherings. The spirits brag about their living loved ones' accomplishments. They request prayers whenever their living loved ones need support. New arrivals to Heaven whose loved ones have been members of these groups will be brought by to visit and to say hello. When I die, I can't wait to attend my grandfather's discussion circle. I want to see all the people who held my hand as they lay dying in the nursing home. To see everyone in perfect health and wholeness, now that's Heavenly!

soul smart tip:

Your beloved people and pets are not "lost" when they die. They support, guide, and love you beyond measure. Remember that energy cannot die; it simply changes form. Love is the most powerful energy in the Universe.
No one is loved more than you!

CHAPTER SIX

children in spirit

THERE IS NO GREATER pain than that of a parent who has lost a child. This is one club that nobody wants to join. I lost count long ago of how many readings I have conducted to connect bereaved parents with their children, and I have also mentored parents so they can begin to make direct connections and can recognize the signs they are receiving from their children.

Even though we have the promise of a Heavenly reunion one day, the pain of having a child go before us is beyond description. If you are a bereaved parent, my heart goes out to you! Only another grieving parent can comprehend what you are feeling, so I recommend that you reach out and find a support group in which bereaved parents together celebrate the lives of their children.

One such group is HelpingParentsHeal.org; I will shortly share more about this wonderful organization.

Based on countless readings, here is some advice for bereaved parents:

- Except in the case of suicide or murder, no one dies before his or her time, so your child's natural death was part of a master plan. Please don't try to force yourself to understand the master plan until after you have returned to Heavenly home.

- If your child died by suicide, please know that children have a much easier time than adults with forgiving themselves for "leaving early." Children respond quickly to the expert, loving care they receive in Heaven.

- Please don't dwell on a traumatic death scene. That is the farthest thing from your child's memories now, and it will lower your vibration, making contact more difficult.

- If your child passed as a baby or a teen, he will not grow older than mid-twenties in spirit. If your child was over thirty at passing, he will appear to be no older than thirty-ish whenever you finally arrive.

- Your child wants to be honored by seeing the family that remains on Earth continuing to live life to the fullest.

- Living people mean well, but they often will say stupid things to you like, "Aren't you over it yet?" I urge you to smile benevolently at the idiots and quickly change the subject. Spend time with others who will accept you, will enjoy talking about your happy memories of your child, and will understand when you need to cry.

- Your child is healthy, happy, and whole on the other side.

- Your child continues to be a part of your family's life.

soul smart tip:

Birthdays, anniversaries, holidays, graduations, weddings, christenings . . . Your child in spirit will be present! Be sure to say, "I love you and I know you are here" often, especially on important dates.

CHILDREN IN SPIRIT HELP EACH OTHER

The spirit world tells us that children organize and help each other to communicate with their families here on Earth. Whenever a child in spirit practices connecting with his family, other children are cheering him on! This leads to the development of new friendships after death. These friends in Heaven can grow very close, to the point where children who have met after death will arrange to have their living parents meet each other. The children want their living parents to support each other and celebrate their children's lives together.

Seven years ago, a delightful young man in spirit unexpectedly entered my life. Ultimately, this young man inspired his mother to co-found an organization named Helping Parents Heal (HelpingParentsHeal.org).

Before Helping Parents Heal ever existed, Morgan Boisson, who is Elizabeth Boisson's son in spirit, arranged for me to meet his mother. That meeting touched off a series of events that led to my introducing Elizabeth to author and afterlife researcher Mark Ireland.

Mark and his wife, Susie, had experienced the devastating transition to the spirit world of their wonderful son, Brandon. Mark had been planning one day to create an organization for grieving parents and families. Together, Mark and Elizabeth founded Helping Parents Heal.

Days after I had met Elizabeth, and although I barely knew her, something made me invite her to visit a potential venue for holding meetings. Soon after, Elizabeth and Mark held their first meeting of the parents support group that was later named Helping Parents Heal. I first volunteered to speak and do readings at the group meeting early on. There were only 40 or 50 members back then.

After I returned home from giving messages at the meeting, I realized that a huge group of happy, joyful children in spirit had followed me. The spirit children said it was their plan for Helping Parents Heal to become a global force for healing families' grief.

I shared the children's message with the parents the next time I volunteered to speak to the group. It seemed as if everyone in that room could feel the children. We knew their message was 100 percent true.

Today, eight years later, HPH has more than 10,000 members worldwide. To learn more, please visit HelpingParentsHeal.org.

To understand how Morgan touched thousands of lives after his physical death, it's time for you to meet his mom, Elizabeth Veney Boisson.

ELIZABETH VENEY BOISSON – IN HER OWN WORDS

On October 20, 2009, my son Morgan died at the Base Camp of Mount Everest in Tibet. It was the most devastating day of my life, but, at the same time it was the moment that I realized that love never dies. I was able to speak to his roommate by cell phone and asked him to put the phone to Morgan's ear. He had stopped breathing and was undergoing CPR. I told him that we loved him, not to be afraid, and that we were very proud of him. At the exact instant that Morgan stopped breathing, I felt him with me, hugging me from the inside. It was a warm, calming feeling that washed through me. I realized that he was comforting me and that he wanted me to know that he would always be with me. Before Morgan died, I did not believe that it would be possible to carry on without one of my children. However, I realized in an instant that I had to carry on, not only for my two daughters who needed me, but more importantly for Morgan, whose only wish is to see us happy. I knew we had to live and thrive for him.

My strongest desire after his death was to somehow communicate with him. I didn't know how this would be possible—I had never been to a medium. Morgan took matters into his own hands.

I had been practicing yoga at a studio for years, and Morgan had sometimes gone with me. Angie, the owner of the studio, decided in January 2010 to interview a medium who had recently moved to the area and was looking for rental space. Angie's way of evaluating the medium, Susanne Wilson, was to ask Susanne to "read" a photo of my kids included in our annual Christmas card. She provided no other information to Susanne.

Susanne connected with my son, communicating his personality and mannerisms. Susanne gave Angie numerous validations—including details that were not public knowledge and not known to Angie (who diligently wrote everything down). I will share a few highlights.

Susanne said a young man showed her a big teddy bear and bottle of Captain Morgan. My son's name is Morgan and we affectionately call him Big Bear. We have a dog named Captain. Susanne saw Morgan shouting through a megaphone that he was OKAY, which was very significant because Morgan was a cheerleader at the University of Arizona and his megaphone was at his service. Susanne saw him on a mountain, lying on his back. She saw a black box at his ear; that he had listened intently but had been unable to speak. He told Susanne to say, "Mom, I heard everything you said and I love you back." I was comforted to know that Morgan had heard me when the phone was held to his ear.

Susanne further told Angie that my son and his two roommates were a "band of three"; that they were like brothers. Although Morgan was close to all the students who helplessly watched him die that morning, his two roommates were especially important to him. Colin and Matt accompanied Morgan's body to Lhasa and waited with him until my husband was able, finally, to get a visa to enter Tibet six days later. Perhaps most stunning—Susanne told Angie that we would receive a special rock from the place that Morgan died and she sketched the rock. We made no mention of this detail to anyone. Several months later Colin delivered Morgan's Rock upon his return from China, exactly as Susanne had said.

A few weeks later, I had my own reading with Susanne in which more validations came through, including that Morgan and I would work together to help parents connect with their deceased children in the Afterlife. Within one month I founded a local parents' support group. Susanne introduced me to Mark Ireland, and with the help of several other bereaved parents we cofounded Helping Parents Heal, which currently has affiliate chapters in several countries.

I know in my heart that Morgan is working diligently in the afterlife to help children get messages through to their parents. I am incredibly proud of him. — **Elizabeth Veney Boisson**

MEET JODY RUFF

Just a few days after I met with Elizabeth, I conducted a phone reading for a lovely woman on the East Coast, named Jody Ruff.

Jody's son, Brian, was an accomplished athlete and a beloved son, brother, and friend. He was also a cadet at the Citadel, The Military College of South Carolina. Before his death, Brian and his friends, all of whom also were Citadel cadets, had planned a road trip. But Brian had a dream in which he "saw" a car accident during the road trip. He warned his friends and asked them to cancel the trip. They went anyway, without Brian, who refused to go. Tragically, all four young men, who had promising futures and families who cherished them, perished in a car accident on that same trip.

Later on, Brian ended his life while sitting in his cherished sports car, a Mustang. His family and friends were utterly devastated.

Now Brian's mother, Jody, was having a reading with me.

Prior to Jody's reading, the only information I had was her first name. I quickly picked up from spirit that Jody was a bereaved mother. Her son, Brian, provided several evidential details, including showing me his Mustang. He introduced his friends, the young men who died in the car accident. Everyone was happy and doing well!

ENTER MORGAN BOISSON

Unexpectedly, I began picking up on another young man who was *not* in the car accident. Standing next to Brian, I spotted Morgan Boisson! I told Jody that a young man named Morgan Boisson was standing next to Brian. Jody was perplexed. She had no clue who Morgan was; bear in mind that Helping Parents Heal did not yet exist.

As the reading continued, I noticed that Morgan seemed to be coaching Brian on communicating with me. Brian was quick to learn, and the two young men seemed to enjoy working together. They both motioned for me to look down at their feet. They were wearing boots, and I heard Brian say that he also had died with his boots on, which his mother then confirmed.

The two young men in spirit motioned for me to look at the scenery around them. They were standing on a hiking path, high atop a mountainside filled with wildflowers. Brian grinned from ear to ear and said, **"Tell my mom we're hiking in Heaven."** At the end of Jody's reading we spoke about the likelihood of Morgan's and Brian's ever meeting while they were in physical form. That probability seemed to be zero.

After Jody's reading, I contacted Elizabeth and told her how Morgan had helped Brian with the reading and that Brian's mom, Jody, was eager to speak with her. Elizabeth and Jody spoke over the phone. Both women were delighted that their sons had met and become friends in Heaven. The words "hiking in Heaven" were significant to Elizabeth because she had been hiking every day without fail since Morgan passed. She had felt his presence every time. Still, the fact that Morgan and Brian were hiking together really didn't mean much to either mom. But that was about to change! **We had no idea that Morgan and Brian in spirit would be connecting next with medium Tina Powers.**

HIKING IN HEAVEN

A few days after I conducted Jody's phone reading in which her son Brian was with Morgan Boisson, Elizabeth went to get a reading in Tucson with medium Tina Powers. Prior to Elizabeth's reading with Tina Powers, one of Elizabeth's daughters had met with Tina. Here I would like to note that although Tina had some limited information about Morgan's death, **Tina Powers knew nothing about Brian Ruff and his connection to Morgan Boisson.**

Now Morgan's mother, Elizabeth, was having a reading with Tina, who observed that there was another young man with Morgan. Tina saw a horse—a Mustang. At first Elizabeth didn't understand, but then she remembered that Brian had transitioned in his car, which was a Ford Mustang. Then Tina mentioned the song "Amazing Grace," one of her symbols for transitioning to the spirit world. Elizabeth understood the connection: Brian had passed in his beloved Mustang. But what Tina said next was astonishing. She said that the two young men were friends, and **"They're hiking in Heaven."**

We mediums never know which details will have the most significance to our clients, so good evidential mediums will give everything that we receive, carefully, without putting our own spin on it.

Tina Powers and I, independently from each other, had simply repeated the words that Brian and Morgan had given us, thereby providing compelling evidence that:

1. The two young men had become friends after death;

2. They had arranged for their mothers to meet;

3. They are thoroughly enjoying their lives after death!

Eight years later, Elizabeth and Jody continue to keep in touch, thanks to their amazing sons, Morgan and Brian!

THE DEAD JOIN US FOR LUNCH

After Elizabeth told me about her reading with Tina, I felt an instant connection to her. I knew I had to meet her, but it took a few months to make arrangements. Elizabeth and I travelled 150 miles to Tucson to meet with Tina at her home. Instantly we felt like old friends. The three of us decided to go out for lunch, and we went to a lovely restaurant where we were seated on the patio. From our table we could see the first row of cars parked in the parking lot along the sidewalk.

The moment we began talking about children in the spirit world, several car alarms went off! First one, then another, and another, until every car in our line of sight had its alarm blaring at full force. There seemed to be no physical explanation. We observed that there was no breeze, and there were no people anywhere near the cars. We sat stunned and speechless for several minutes as people from the restaurant came running out to their cars and shut off their car alarms.

A minute after the last person had shut off his car alarm, all the car alarms started going off again! I looked at Tina and Elizabeth. We were all stunned. Then Tina giggled and gave a funny little snort, so I started laughing. Elizabeth was laughing, too. Our laughter and all those car alarms made it sound like quite a party, and we merrily toasted all our friends in spirit who had joined us that day!
Insert new paragraph because this just happened :)

I was honored recently to give a keynote address at the first Helping Parents Heal conference, along with three other keynote speakers: George Anderson, Suzanne Giesemann, and Dr. Gary Schwartz. I shared the story of Brian's and Morgan's meeting and arranging for their mothers on Earth to become friends. If you're a parent of a child who is living in Heaven, pay close attention to other bereaved parents who enter your life.

I have heard many accounts of spirit children arranging for their families who are here on Earth to meet. Children, who are living on the "other side of life," want their families, here on Earth, to become friends and have fun. They are thrilled when their families gather and celebrate the greater reality: that love lives forever and relationships need never end. When families gather, especially for an outing, a meal, or something fun, the children gather too. They will be right there, with you!

CHILDREN WHO DIE VERY YOUNG

Many times during readings, the spirit child who is communicating with me will say something like, "Remember, Mommy, you had a feeling that I might not live very long." The children want to reassure their parents that there was nothing that could have been done to keep them from dying young. I have met bereaved parents who felt guilty because they had a feeling or a knowing that their child was going to die young. After the child died, they felt guilty because maybe those feelings had been a warning and they had been meant to do something to prevent the death.

On the contrary, the reason the living parent had that odd feeling is that the early death of the child was part of a plan. **This "knowing" is not to make the parent feel responsible for preventing the death, but rather it is to acknowledge on a soul level that the young child's death was going to happen in accordance with a plan.** The knowing doesn't come with a time and date of the upcoming death, and if you think about it, that makes sense. After all, if the teacher gave us all the answers to the test questions, how would we learn? It is very difficult for some parents to accept that each soul has a plan. This plan outlines the broad strokes of a life designed to deliver what the souls involved need in order to grow. Death is a part of everyone's plan. But it is exponentially more difficult to get through a death when the loved one is a cherished child.

I've heard many people say that the child who died young had a special quality, an "old soul" feeling. There was something different about the old-soul child; you could see it in his or her eyes. And the spirit world has affirmed the truth behind this statement. Often the child was truly an advanced soul who volunteered to take on the assignment of living a brief life, and the child's transition at a young age was intended to help specific souls on Earth to accomplish their own spiritual growth objectives.

MANY TEACHER SOULS TRANSITION YOUNG

Powerful teacher souls who come to Earth and die as children will often go the extra mile to appear as post-death apparitions. They seem to have such a high vibration that others who are non-mediums can see them, and they appear to be flesh and blood, as real as you or I. This was the case with a wonderful young man named Aleksander Mirkovic. Six people, all non-mediums and independently of the others, have seen Aleksander's apparition. And in all six sightings, the individuals described the same distinctive clothing that Aleksander wore.

I first met Aleksander's mother, Katarina, when I was attending a book signing in Mountain View, California. I wasn't scheduled to speak. I was there to watch. Just before the event started, Katarina arrived. Instantly, she recognized me in the audience and gave me a hug. I asked Katarina if I had ever done a reading for her. She said that she hadn't been able to get an appointment with me because hundreds were waiting. Still, she expressed her gratitude for the mediumship work I do. I felt honored and touched by her words. But there was no further time to chat. The presentation was about to begin.

The speaker invited me to talk briefly about how to recognize signs from loved ones in spirit. But the spirit world had other plans! **I saw a young man in spirit standing directly behind Katarina.** He was wearing a purple sleeveless jersey, the kind that basketball players wear, and a kitchen apron over the jersey. It seemed to be an odd combination, but it made perfect sense to Katarina. I gave Katarina an impromptu reading, including what Aleksander was wearing, as well as the fact that he said, "Tell my mother I am in the kitchen with her all the time, and I hug her!"

Katarina confirmed that she and her family owned a restaurant, and her son, Aleksander, had been loved by all the customers. The reason he appeared wearing a purple basketball jersey and apron was that he had hoped to play for the Los Angeles Lakers one day, but he also loved working in the family's restaurant. I had to leave to catch a plane back to Phoenix, so the rest of the messages would need to wait. I could tell there would be much more to come since Aleksander had brought "D.D.," his pet name for his grandfather and Katarina's dad.

When later I connected with Katarina, her son Aleksander showed up with his grandfather and several other relatives in spirit. Katarina's father showed me that he had been a respected artist in

Serbia, the family's native country. He was excited about his current project in Heaven, a sculpture that he was creating by hand of a Mount Rushmore-sized bust of Master Jesus. Katarina confirmed that her father had sculpted a bust of Master Jesus in life, and always had wanted to make a bigger one!

Aleksander told me he was six feet, five inches tall, which Katarina confirmed. He went on to confirm a long list of signs that he had given to his family, and Katarina checked them off one by one as correct. Aleksander said that he was concerned about basketball players, and he wanted to thank his family for helping them. I was puzzled, but Katarina explained that Aleksander had died from Marfan syndrome, a connective tissue disorder that is often found in the basketball athletic community. Those who have Marfan syndrome grow very tall and thin, which can help them to be great basketball players but also causes numerous other symptoms. Since Aleksander's death, Katarina's family had raised money to give scholarships to basketball players at the community college which their son had attended. They had also worked to draw attention to the need for more research to find a cure for Marfan syndrome. Aleksander explained that he, too, was doing his part from spirit to cure Marfan. He has established a team of powerful souls in spirit who are working to inspire living scientists and philanthropists to adequately fund research so a cure can be developed. And knowing how powerful and determined Aleksander is, a cure is going to be just a matter of time!

MISCARRIED BABIES

Parents of a miscarried baby are sometimes curious about what happened to their baby's soul when the fetus died. The answer is that the soul is kept safely in the spirit world and does not experience the death. Until the baby is born, the soul lives primarily in the spirit world but it is free to come and go from its fetal physical body at will. It is said to be a wonderfully contented feeling, unlike any other, for the soul to feel what it is like to be a fetus inside the womb. The feeling of being in the womb is an experience that is impossible to duplicate in the spirit world. If you miscarried a baby, you have something wonderful to look forward to, because one day when you transition Home you will find a beautiful young adult who adores you!

What is the purpose of a miscarriage? The spirit world tells us there are a couple of reasons why a miscarriage might be necessary. First, the miscarriage could have happened in service to the spiritual progress of one or both parents. Another possibility is that for whatever reason the soul changed its mind about being born. The spirits teach us that the soul who wasn't born into a family due to miscarriage is often born into the same family line at a later date.

Recently I was doing a reading for a woman who had miscarried several times. Earlier she had been incapacitated by grief, and she had cursed God for her losses. After years of therapy, she had begun a discipline of journaling, prayer, and meditation. Eventually she had accepted her life as it was, so she had become a happy person again, and she partook fully in life. She hadn't given up, but she had decided to love herself and live fully in spite of her inability to give birth.

My heart hurt for this woman, but she was spiritually strong and I knew she could handle whatever information came through. Of course, she wanted to know if she would ever have a baby.

Immediately a masculine spirit appeared to me. He explained that he wasn't born previously because of an agreement he and his mother had made as souls. He went on to explain that all her miscarriages had been in service to her soul's growth. Through the losses, she had gained the opportunity to learn to love and not blame herself. She also had learned to accept help from others in her darkest hours. These were lessons that she had tried, over many lifetimes, to bring to fruition.

The soul of her future son then said, "You will see me next year." Wow! Although that was wonderful news for my client, I can't tell you how nervous I felt about promising her that she would become pregnant and carry a son to full term by next year. Quickly I asked my spiritual team if they felt I could trust this information, and I received all three of the usual "positive" responses from my team (thumbs up, green light, and the happy "ding, ding, ding" of a bell). So I gave this information to my client, who was pleased to hear it, open-minded yet skeptical, and rightfully so.

Later that year, my client left me a message that she had indeed become pregnant that fall. The following summer I received the birth announcement for her baby boy. Her son, who is now in school, is the light of her life.

BEST FRIEND FOREVER

The next event is deeply personal to me. I hope that in my sharing it, someone who has lost a child to a devastating disease will take some comfort from it.

One of my closest childhood friends was Blake, a boy my

age who attended our church. He was always telling silly jokes and making faces so people would smile. When it would be time to go home, we always had a ritual: one of us would say, "See you later, alligator," and the other would answer, "After a while, crocodile."

We were both nine years old when Blake was diagnosed with a cancerous brain tumor. There was little hope. I visited him in the hospital after he had surgery. He didn't look good at all, yet I never doubted that I would see him again. A few weeks passed. I was watching television in the playroom when Blake walked in with a big smile on his face. Finally, I had my friend back! I had known all along that he would get well. I told him to come on in; a good television show was on. Blake plopped down on the bean bag chair right next to mine. Boy oh boy, it was good to have my friend back! Our happy reunion did not last long.

A moment later, my grandfather came in, looking solemn. There were tears on his cheeks as he told me he had bad news. Blake had passed away that day; Granddad had been with Blake and his parents when he died. My head swung toward the beanbag chair where Blake had sat down. Now the chair was empty.

I did not attend Blake's funeral. For once, I didn't go to a funeral that my grandfather conducted because I would have cried like a baby. I was only nine years old. I soon regretted not going, since at least I would have seen Blake there. I really needed to see my friend. I wanted to know that he was okay!

Weeks passed. There was no sign of Blake. You see, a medium cannot order a spirit person to appear. A medium has to do the same thing you would do: invite your beloved spirit person to make a connection and then set up all the right conditions to help them connect.

Finally, one night lying in bed, I had an idea.

"See you later, alligator," I said in my mind.

There was no reply. Swallowing disappointment, I tried again. Only this time, I said it out loud as if I really meant it: "See you later, alligator!"

"After a while, crocodile," Blake shot right back. He was okay! He had answered me!

Since then, I have seen Blake in spirit many times. He accompanies children who have died from cancer whenever the child's family is having a reading with me. Blake coaches the child regarding how to get messages through to me in the best way.

soul smart tip:

In readings while helping children communicate with their families, Blake has assured many parents that their child has no memory of having suffered the disease. All the child remembers is the cuddles, laughter, and love.

I am not the only person who has seen Blake.

Bear in mind that I've never written about or discussed Blake with anyone outside of my immediate family but, during mediumship mentoring sessions, two of my students at different times have spontaneously seen the spirit of a young male in my office. They both said he wanted to say hello. The young man appeared to be in his twenties, which is the age that Blake prefers to be. They said he died from cancer. One student went further, saying that he was my childhood friend. Then she gave his first name with no prompting from me (I have changed his name for this book). She said that his presence made her smile.

part two

MEDIUMSHIP FOR NON-MEDIUMS: REGULAR PEOPLE CONNECTING WITH THEIR LOVED ONES IN SPIRIT

—— CHAPTER SEVEN ——

how the dead send and receive messages

COMMUNICATION BETWEEN THE LIVING and the dead is natural, but still it is not easy. In fact, after-death communication is so challenging that both the living and the dead must learn and practice their techniques. There are schools that teach the dead how to communicate with the living, and schools that teach the living how to communicate with the dead.

Please know that the souls in the spirit world want to speak with their living loved ones every bit as much as we want to speak with them. While you are reading this book, one of your beloved spirit people might be reading over your shoulder. Remember, they study up on things, too! It can be helpful to know what a loved one in spirit is actually doing behind the scenes to communicate with you, since by understanding what they need you may be able to help them to better get through to you!

DRESS REHEARSALS

The Halls of Reunion have staging areas dedicated to helping the spirits rehearse how they will connect with their living loved ones. For them, it's live theater! There are stages for merging their energy with that of a butterfly, dragonfly, or bird. And other stages for doing practice dream visits and meditation visits. Higher vibrational beings—you might think of them as angels or extraterrestrials—lend their support as coaches and as gatekeepers between the worlds. They are volunteers who find pleasure in doing this work.

The spirits thoroughly enjoy planning, rehearsing, and executing meditation visits and dream visits. Of course, they are excited about visiting with their loved ones on the Earth plane. But if the living loved one is still in the throes of extreme grief, it might not be possible to make the connection. Patience is required, since grief lowers the living person's vibration so much that it can obscure or temporarily block the connection.

If you follow the advice coming up for meeting your loved one in meditation, something amazing happens. The staging area inside the Hall of Reunion will become an exact duplicate of the place that you envision for your meditation visit. And then when it's ready, the meeting place that you have helped to construct energetically in a Hall of Reunion will be moved onto the astral plane. Here, your consciousness and your loved one's consciousness will ultimately meet during your meditation visit.

soul smart tip:

The more clearly you can visualize or imagine the meeting place, the more realistic the stage can be made, as if it were a movie set. You will be synchronizing your vibration with that of your loved one in spirit.

The actual meeting with your loved one, whether it happens in your meditation or your dream, will take place within a dimension somewhere between the Earth plane and the spirit world. This is what we refer to as the astral plane. Remember that an aspect of your consciousness will temporarily go out of body for this meeting. If you follow the instructions coming up, you won't really have to think about going out of body. It will happen!

By the way, if you would like to know more about the astral plane and how to travel out of body to the astral from Earth, I recommend the work of Robert Monroe, founder of the Monroe Institute, and Jurgen Ziewe. Also, check out author Cyrus Kirkpatrick, an emerging expert regarding out-of-body experiences.

LITTLE BIRD, BIG MESSAGE

In early April of 2016 I was meeting with Dr. Gary Schwartz on a video conference call. Gary is a Professor of Psychology, Medicine, Neurology, Psychiatry, and Surgery, and, as if that were not enough he is also the Director of the Laboratory for Advances in Consciousness and Health at the University of Arizona in Tucson. He has published several hundred scientific papers, and written books about various kinds of scientific evidence related to the survival of consciousness. I am honored to work as a volunteer research medium with Gary and his gifted wife, Rhonda Eklund Schwartz, who also is a medium. Through this work, I have met fascinating people both living and dead, and I have had some amazing experiences! For example, not long ago Gary and Rhonda invited me to stay at the home of the late science fiction icon, Forrest Ackerman. We were with a diversely talented group including my long-time friend, medium Jamie Clark; professor H. Dieter Steklis and Netzin Steklis; producer and filmmaker Paul Jeffrey Davids; professor John Allison; and the prolific paranormal author, Rosemary Ellen Guiley and her husband, Joe Redmiles. You can learn more about the Ackermansion investigation in the book, *An Atheist in Heaven*.

As my video conference call with Gary on that April day in 2016 was ending, somehow the topic came up of how the spirits use birds and insects to send us signs. I said that what amazes me most is how the spirits make it happen. One of their favorite methods is to use a device that looks like a remote control! In several of my readings, and in conversations with trusted friends in the spirit world, I have been shown that sometimes, although not always, they like to use these special remote-control devices to control the movements of the birds or insects in order to give a sign. Before that happens, the spirit telepathically asks the bird or insect for permission. Once the soul-to-soul connection has been established, they use the remote-control device to give the bird or insect precise maneuvers to impress the living person that it's a sign!

After the sign has been given, the spirit and the bird or insect disconnect their soul-to-soul connection. The bird or insect who volunteered to help seems to experience a surge of positive energy that may linger for hours afterward. A nice reward!

Of course, Gary is a scientist so he listened that day and replied with his characteristic, "Hmm." That was what I expected: not excitement, but just a "Hmm," since this is anecdotal information and not intended to be scientific data. Then Gary surprised me! He said that he had recently heard very similar comments from another medium named Suzanne Giesemann. I didn't know her, but now I wanted to meet her. And I was about to get that opportunity in an unexpected way.

Three weeks after that meeting with Gary Schwartz, I was finishing up a day of work at my office and hurrying to change clothes to attend an event. Part of the event would include an early evening hike in the Sonoran Desert foothills close by. But this was no ordinary hike; it was, instead, part of a ceremony to dedicate park benches as memorials to two young men who had died. The young men were Morgan Boisson (you read about Morgan in Chapter 6) and Kyle Erikson, the wonderful young son of Glenn and Nita Erickson.

Just as I was leaving my office, I thought about the two young men. They must be excited about their bench dedication! I asked, "Morgan, are you around? Are you coming on the hike?" I didn't receive an immediate answer, and time was pressing, so I headed for the door. That was when I heard loud tapping sounds. I followed the tapping sounds, and I realized that something was tapping on the window directly across from my desk. The blinds were closed, so I opened them and, to my surprise there was a cactus wren there was a cactus wren sitting on the ledge of my office window, tapping.

Not only wasn't the little bird afraid, but it quickly became clear it was trying to communicate! "Is that you, Morgan?" I asked aloud as I placed my fingertips on the glass. The bird turned his head slightly to the side and pressed his cheek against the glass on the exact spot where my fingertips rested. We held that position for more than a minute, which is a pretty long time for a wild bird and a human to be so close to one another. Finally the bird sat up again, but it didn't leave the ledge. It continued to look directly at me. Then, thinking of the other young man, Kyle, I asked aloud, "Kyle, are you here too?" Before I could finish the sentence, a woodpecker appeared and sat next to the cactus wren! I said, "Hi Kyle, thank you!" I watched the birds in awe for a while as they simply stared back at me. I told them thank you and goodbye, then left for the dedication ceremony.

Dozens of people showed up for the ceremony. When all the hikers had arrived at the benches, Morgan's mother, Elizabeth, introduced me to Suzanne Giesemann. She was the medium I wanted to meet! I can't tell you how wonderful it was to have a kindred soul, another medium, there at this beautiful and emotionally-charged event. I saw spirit children as well as angels gathered with us. We enjoyed the waves of unconditional love that washed over us, and we felt the love of Morgan and Kyle!

Suzanne and I were chatting in my office two days later when we both heard tapping on my office window. That cactus wren was back at the exact same spot! Here, I would like to point out that my office consists of three rooms, all of which have multiple large windows, but the bird chose a particular spot on the window that perfectly matched a direct line of sight from my chair. This time, both Suzanne and I were able to connect with the bird by placing our fingertips on the glass while the bird touched the glass with his beak or with the side of his head exactly where our fingertips were. The experience made us both smile.

For all of that next day I kept glancing at my office window to see if the little bird would appear again, but there was no sign of it until 5:10 pm. This time the bird would not stop tapping, even when I pressed my fingertips to the glass. It was an insistent, robotic regular tapping that lasted for a full fifteen minutes, after which the bird flew away. It never returned. It didn't feel like Morgan or Kyle this time, and frankly, I was a bit annoyed by the persistent noise since I cherish the peace and quiet at my office.

But what happened next was amazing!

A **little after 6:00 p.m. I received a text from Suzanne Giesemann.** She asked me if anything had happened that day, because she had been conducting an experiment of which I was unaware. I texted her back that, yes, something did happen: that little bird came back, but the bird's behavior was quite different from what it had been when it was being controlled by Morgan's spirit two days earlier. I explained that the bird had tapped incessantly for fifteen minutes. Suzanne asked me at what time this had happened. I replied, "About 5:10 p.m." She then texted me a screen capture of a notation she had made at 5:00 p.m. that day, stating that she had begun an experiment. Okay, Suzanne, what experiment? I was ready for the punch line.

Suzanne explained that she had intended to "send a portion of my own soul to visit you, as I had been reading a Seth book and he mentioned that one can send his own soul to actually materialize in front of others. I thought that if anyone could sense this presence, it would be you." She later added that when she had sent her soul to me,

Suzanne had thought, *"Hi, Susanne. It's me. Can you see me?"*

I discussed Suzanne's experiment with a trusted friend, author and afterlife researcher Craig Hogan. He pointed out that when Suzanne sent a piece of her soul to me, she did not choose the cactus wren or try to control the outcome. She set a clear intention, and her spiritual team assisted. They must have known that the cactus wren would get my attention. **Always remember that spirit communication is like water: it will travel the path of least resistance. Keep your heart and mind open, and pay attention to whatever is getting your attention!**

soul smart tip:

Your loved ones in spirit can see you when you "send your soul" temporarily to meet with them! Here is a list of several ways to make it happen:

First, when you think of your loved one in spirit, he or she can receive your thought.

It is helpful to say the name (first name will do), and then think the thought that you want to send. Or say it out loud. For example, say, "Cindy, it's me. I just wanted to say I'm thinking about you and I love you." Depending upon how Cindy prefers to receive my thought, she will hear it in my voice; but she may also see my thought like a little pop-up window that appears in her aura next to her, where she can read it as well.

Second, when you talk out loud to your loved ones in spirit, they are delighted.

This gives them bragging rights! It's a source of pride that you do this for them. They will receive your message in much the same way that we receive voicemail. In Heaven, some say it is easier to hear you more clearly when you speak to them out loud.

Third, when you wish to send a card or note to a loved one in spirit, you can act on that desire.

Go ahead—buy your loved ones birthday cards and write letters to them. When you are finished writing, seal the envelope and write your loved one's name on it. Next, hold it to your heart for a moment, saying the name, and adding that you have a card or a note for them: "Hi Bob! I love you and I'm sending you this card!" As amazing as this sounds, your loved one will receive it! In fact, we have been told, time and time again, that an exact duplicate will be delivered to them. And some of them will be so excited that they can't wait; they will read over your shoulder even before you have finished!

If you're wondering what to do afterwards with the card or letter, you can keep it, although there is an exception if your letter concerns forgiveness. **If you are requesting forgiveness from your loved one, or if you are giving forgiveness to your loved one in spirit, it is advisable to shred or burn the note when you are truly ready to let it go.** Then only the love will remain. It may surprise you to find how much lighter you feel after you have released the burden of needing to give or to accept forgiveness. Your loved one will feel better, too!

Now, are you ready to meet your loved one in meditation? Great! Let's turn the page.

———— CHAPTER EIGHT ————

centering yourself

EVERYONE HAS THE POTENTIAL to communicate with his or her own loved ones in spirit. This is part of your birthright as a child of The Creator. For years I have been mentoring people in developing this ability, and I find that the number-one roadblock people will experience is fear. I want you to ask yourself this question: "Am I afraid, even in the slightest bit, to connect with my loved one in spirit?"

If your answer is "yes," you are not alone. Fear can create a barrier to mediumship for many non-mediums. You must give yourself permission to experience a new kind of relationship with your loved ones who have passed. However, some people worry that by opening up to good spirits, they may inadvertently connect with bad ones, even though the chances of that are just about zero. But the more common fear is failure to make the connection; we don't want to risk piling disappointment onto our grief. **The good news is that with just a bit of practice, these fears can melt away and you can develop a new type of relationship with your loved one in spirit.**

Here's a cautionary tale to illustrate how fear can get in the way. But don't worry; there is a happy ending!

THE WIDOW NEEDS A SIGN

A few years ago I was conducting a reading by phone for Dorothy, a widow in the Midwestern U.S. Although I don't open up to spirit until fifteen minutes before a reading, occasionally a spirit person will show up early at my house. This is what happened on the morning of Dorothy's phone reading. While I was putting on my makeup, I felt a man in spirit who was eager to connect with his romantic love. I had two readings and one student scheduled that day. I told the spirit man, "Thank you for coming; now please go to my office and please speak up when your great love is having the reading."

The instant that Dorothy and I connected on the phone, her husband in spirit, Ted, wasted no time in connecting with me. His energy was like a cozy blanket, and he felt like a doting husband. Immediately I knew that Ted and Dorothy had been the center of each other's worlds. Ted showed me his death, as spirit people often will do. He had been watching a baseball game on TV when he had been hit by a massive stroke and died quickly. I am very descriptive when giving a reading, since the details are a big part of the message.

I told Dorothy that I felt her husband's loving presence, and that he had been watching a baseball game on TV when he had passed suddenly. Ted was wearing a red and white t-shirt, and the baseball team wore red and white uniforms. Immediately, I felt Dorothy relax into the reading. "Nobody knows about the baseball game or what Ted was wearing," she said.

"Well, your husband certainly remembers." I smiled.

Then I heard the words, "Tell my wife . . . I don't want to scare her." I was puzzled, but it isn't my job to figure out what the message means. The medium is simply the messenger. So I repeated the message that her husband didn't want to scare her.

Dorothy gasped, "Of course! It makes sense now." She then explained that she had been asking Ted every day to give her a sign to show that he was with her. Months had passed without a sign. Dorothy quickly explained, "I've been asking Ted to send me a sign. But I always add, 'Please don't scare me!' Don't you see? My husband was always protecting me. I'm not getting signs because he's worried he will scare me." Ted gave me a "thumbs up" to indicate that Dorothy was correct.

Dorothy promised Ted that she would figure out how to let go of her fear. I promised both Ted and Dorothy that I would help. After the reading ended, I shared with Dorothy how to go about grounding and protection. I gave her an audio copy of my five-minute meditation, The Daily Peace, to help her become centered and unafraid, so she could ask for and receive signs from her husband without fear.

A few months later, I received a card with a bright red cardinal on the front. Inside was a handwritten note from Dorothy. She was happy to report that she was no longer afraid, and that she now received regular signs from Ted. A cardinal had appeared at her kitchen window on Ted's birthday, and the bird had returned several times since, at special moments. And what about the red and white uniforms of the baseball team, and the matching t-shirt Ted had been wearing when he died? That had been Ted's favorite team, the St. Louis Cardinals.

soul smart tip:

Being grounded and protected is like putting a burglar alarm sticker on the front of your house. Chances are that you'll never need your burglar alarm, but if a burglar should come to your neighborhood you can bet that he'll skip the house with the alarm in favor of the house without it. Burglars don't want to work too hard, and they certainly don't want to get caught! And the same applies to negative entities: they will skip you when they see that you have surrounded yourself with protective energies. Dealing with you will be too much work. They will quickly move on and find a hateful person who has negative thoughts and a vibratory level that is closer to their own.

soul smart tip:

You must give yourself permission to experience a new kind of relationship with your loved ones in spirit. Release your fears; you are safe. It is your loving thoughts, good intentions, and gratitude that give you the best grounding and protection of all. By saying a brief grounding and protection prayer, you are setting the intention to stay within the power of love, which is the highest vibration in the Universe.

If you should ever sense an energy around you that doesn't feel positive, a quick way to banish that energy is to draw three clockwise circles using your hand in the general area where you sense the energy, and command it to leave. Just draw the three clockwise circles in front of you if you feel a negative energy but you don't know which direction it might be coming from. But again, nothing like this should happen unless you are a paranormal investigator who is out visiting haunted locations. By the way, I generally won't take a new student who does paranormal investigations, because I don't want to get myself involved with any entities that might have followed that investigator home! But you are safe in connecting with your own loved ones.

Back to grounding and protection: Please feel free to use any protection words or prayers that resonate with you. Or you can use a protection bubble, create your own protection method, or else use a traditional prayer or poem. Keep your protection prayer brief, and use words that resonate in your heart so the intention will be strong.

Here are some options. From Christianity, we have The Lord's Prayer or Psalm 23 ("The Lord is My Shepherd"). From Kabbalah (Jewish mysticism), we have *Ana Bekoach* or *Ben Porat Yosef.* You can say the prayer in your mother tongue, but keep a printed copy in the original Hebrew nearby. You may also visualize a grounding cord that extends from your root chakra at the base of your spine (or from under your seat) and goes deep into Mother Earth, thereby keeping you grounded and centered.

The following is a suggested protection prayer that I have used for years, and of course you are welcome to use it as well.

An expanded five-minute protection prayer, *The Daily Peace,* is included in Appendix A of this book. You also can purchase *The Daily Peace* as a download on my website, CarefreeMedium.com.

GOLDEN BUBBLE OF PROTECTION

Divine Source (or Holy Creator or God),
Thank you for blessing me with this day, with my life, and with
my many blessings.
Thank you for giving me another opportunity to serve you in
this body.
I ask that you surround me in a beautiful, translucent golden bubble
of protection
That is bathed in the divine white light of your holy spirit,
Sealing IN all of my positive energies and good health,
Sealing OUT all negative energies, ill health and entities from
lower realms,
And I send white light to the lower realms,
So that only peace, love, and protection may enter in.
I ask also that you surround <say loved ones' names>, each
in a beautiful translucent golden bubble of protection
That is bathed in the divine white light of your holy spirit,
Sealing IN all of their positive energies and good health,
Sealing OUT all negative energies, ill health and entities from
lower realms,
So that only peace, love, and protection may enter in.
And so it is!

Here is a prayer that you may have heard previously. It is beautiful in its simplicity.

PRAYER FOR PROTECTION BY JAMES DILLET FREEMAN

The light of God surrounds me;
The love of God enfolds me;
The power of God protects me;
The presence of God watches over me;
Wherever I am, God is!

soul smart tip:

After you have given yourself permission, being centered is the next step in connecting with loved ones in spirit. To be centered, keep your thoughts and intentions loving and positive. Create or borrow a brief grounding and protection prayer and use it daily. You have control over the energies around you, so there is nothing for you to fear.

——— CHAPTER NINE ———

building up your power

WE HAVE TALKED ABOUT giving yourself permission to connect with spirit and becoming centered and grounded. The next step is to build your personal spiritual power, and allow the divine light to flow through you. When mediums are taught to do this, it is called "sitting in the power."

You must treat yourself with kindness. This is an integral part of building your power! At this very moment, your consciousness resides mainly in the spirit world with only a portion of your consciousness operating your body through your brain. Think of a computer. Your brain is the operating system, but your consciousness writes the code that programs your brain. If you feel run down or depressed, begin today to make whatever changes are necessary so you can operate better.

This means having good nutrition with mostly whole foods, eight hours or more of sleep nightly, and quiet time in your home. I'm going to share some easy ways to build up your personal, spiritual power. Everything recommended here is intended to help you raise your vibration to more easily connect with loved ones in spirit. And there is a bonus: you could end up living a healthier and happier life!

You may not realize that your loved ones in spirit must use YOUR energy to connect with you. You are a large part of their power source; it is your "love focus" that helps your vibration to align with theirs. To give you the proper perspective, it is time to talk about energy centers in your body. Chakras! Now, there is a hippy-dippy word for you, right? I'll ask you to bear with me anyway, and I promise to give you only the information you need; we won't go too far down the rabbit-hole.

YOUR ENERGY CENTERS

Perhaps you have practiced yoga or studied energy healing options, such as Reiki. You may have heard the term "chakra" discussed in class. Chakra is a Sanskrit word that means "wheel." The human body contains tens of thousands of chakras. These are energy wheels or energy centers that correspond to nerves, plexuses, and organs within the physical body. They also are associated with intuition, communication, creativity, and empowerment in the non-physical body.

Your chakras, or energy centers, act as power sources for you to manifest your life. And you co-create your life with the Universe based on your free will, including all your thoughts, words, and actions.

Your loved ones in the light tap into your chakra power when they communicate with you, and to the medium's chakra power when you are having a reading. They actually connect up their energies to your energies. They do this mainly through your heart chakra, which is located in the middle of your chest, and through your solar plexus chakra, which is a couple of inches above your naval.

The solar plexus is your center of personal power. Mediumship requires a strong solar plexus. This "fire in the belly" provides the power for all the chakras above the solar plexus, and those are the ones that give you the three main clairs: clairvoyance (clear seeing); claircognizance (clear knowing); and clairaudience (clear hearing). Have you ever seen a sparkly "spirit light" in your peripheral vision? If so, it's likely that a loved one in spirit has tapped into the power of your third-eye chakra so you could see their presence. And the third-eye isn't really an eye, of course; it's a chakra located in the middle of your forehead.

Have you ever thought you heard the voice of your loved one in spirit? It might sound like a clear, spontaneous thought that simply pops into your head. If so, your loved one was tapping into the power of your throat chakra, which is the energy center for hearing spirit.

HOW TO BALANCE AND RECHARGE CHAKRAS

So, how can you keep your chakras strong? By maintaining a positive outlook, getting enough rest, and eating whole foods that are of high nutritional value and low density; in other words, more fruits and vegetables and fewer animal products. If you are a worrier, you must stop it now! Worrying creates negative thoughts that manifest through the chakras into your body as sickness and pain. You already know that a sick person with a positive attitude heals faster. Well, a positive attitude also powers up your connection with the spirit world.

soul smart tip:

Grief over the death of a loved one will weaken the chakras temporarily. This is one of the reasons why I recommend waiting at least ninety days, or however long it takes before your most extreme grief has lightened a bit, before having a reading with a professional medium. You might want to look into Reiki or yoga for healing the effects of grief on the body.

Once the worst part of your grief is over, try to get yourself back to center emotionally. Concentrate on appreciating the precious time that you had with your loved one! For those experiencing extreme grief, I recommend that you visit Mark Pitstick's website, SoulProof.com. You will find resources to navigate through this time in your life and return to your center.

soul smart tip:

When your extreme grief finally settles down into bittersweet memories, your chakras will take on extra power because you have survived and you are ready to thrive! This is mainly why intuitive and mediumship abilities sometimes emerge AFTER the death of someone who was close to you. Allowing yourself to

honor your grief by fully experiencing it rather than denying it will help you to build your personal power. Live your life to the fullest, even though you still miss your loved one.

SYNERGY PEACE: MANIFEST HEALTH AND SERENITY

For years, my students have been using a twenty-two-minute meditation that I designed to balance and recharge one's chakras. I'm giving you a free copy of the meditation script in the Appendices. You may use the script to make your own audio recording and play it back during your meditation. Or purchase this meditation with my narration and accompanied by composer John Vhames on Native American flute at CarefreeMedium.com.

SITTING IN THE POWER

Sitting in the power is an exercise intended to prepare you to connect with spirit, but it is not connecting with loved ones in the light. It is a way to remember that you have the spark of God, the divine light, always within you, and that you are always connected to it. It is a technique to raise your vibration.

My favorite way to sit in the power is to begin by tracing Reiki symbols with my hand in the air in front of me, but you can skip this step if you haven't been attuned to Reiki.

Then close your eyes and visualize a spark of intensely white light at either your heart chakra or your middle section near your solar plexus chakra and abdomen. With practice, you will have a sense of whether you prefer visualizing the light at your middle section or your heart.

Visualize this light expanding to fill your body, and then expanding to fill the room.

Next, visualize a bigger, more intense white light appearing above your head. This bigger light outside your body represents the Source, or whatever label you might prefer to give to the energy that connects you to the Creator and to all the Universe.

Remember, you are NOT connecting with spirits right now! You are connecting to Source energy. There are many ways to visualize merging the light that is inside of you with all the love and light in the Universe. I advise you to keep it simple, and remember that you only need five or ten minutes for sitting in the power, although you are welcome to sit as long as you like.

soul smart tip:

After you have done your grounding and protection, sit in the power for a little while before you begin connecting with loved ones. This means visualizing the bright white light within you merging with an even brighter light that is the Source energy.

CREATING PHYSICAL SACRED SPACE

We have talked about creating the sacred space within. Next, do you have a relaxing place in your home for meditation? If not, please do yourself a favor and create it. Your sacred space can be simple or ornate; it can be indoors, perhaps in your living room, or outdoors in your garden or on your patio. When choosing the place, remember that it is better always to meditate in the same place so you can take advantage of the accumulation of positive energies. The energy of love and peace will imprint over time wherever you meditate. That's why visiting a church can be so uplifting, even if you are not really religious: over time, many positive energies have melded into the walls, floors, furniture, and even down into the foundation of the church, mosque, synagogue, or other place of positive worship. When you use it regularly, your meditation place will begin to feel like a sacred space, regardless of how simple you make it.

If you normally work from home, please sit in a chair other than your work chair. Perhaps an exercise or yoga mat will work better for you. If you are going to use a candle, crystals, or other materials, it's fine to keep them out for others to see. If you decide to put them away after you meditate, use a special container for storage so that it, too, becomes sacred space.

I like to have lots of natural light in my sacred space. I use a comfortable chair and a small coffee table. In the beginning of my meditation practice, I used only one white candle and nothing else; that seemed to be enough. Over the years, though, I have added things to my table that have meaning to me. Your sacred meditation space should be personalized for you! Mine has miniature pictures of Master Jesus, Mother Mary, and Archangel Michael; an angel figurine; a Buddha figurine; and several crystals, many of which are heart-shaped. I also use essential oils including rosemary and eucalyptus oils in a diffuser to enhance focus, increase clarity, and raise my vibration. I spray rosewater in the air and on my heart chakra, directly onto the skin at the middle of the chest for enhancing the soul-to-soul connection with the spirit world. Burning incense or sage is helpful every so often, mainly to clear out what I call "spiritual dust bunnies," which are stagnant energies that can build up over time.

If you can't be in your sacred space but you wish to meditate, try to find a comfortable place outdoors with Mother Nature. Alternatively, from wherever you are—even sitting on an airplane— you can visualize or imagine that you are at home, sitting in your sacred space while you meditate. I have done this on a bumpy plane ride and it gave me peace. Meditation on a plane is better for you than having a cocktail to stay calm.

soul smart tip:

Your beloved spirit people and people and pets will use your energy centers as their power source, so you must take good care of yourself both mentally and physically, for their sake as much as for your own. This includes keeping yourself strong and balanced, and your environment as peaceful and relaxing as possible. Feel free to experiment with essential oils and crystals to find what works best for you. You cannot make a mistake because it is your intention that matters most!

PAY ATTENTION TO WHAT'S GETTING YOUR ATTENTION

Have you ever wondered if those same numbers that you often see are being sent to you by spirit? Sending you numbers as a sign is one of the most common ways the spirit world catches your attention. I am told that guides, angels, and beloved spirit people and pets all enjoy sending numbers to their beloved living people. The numbers are themselves a friendly reminder that those in spirit who adore you are continually helping behind the scenes.

If you're keeping a journal, keep track of the numbers that catch your attention. Which numbers do you see over and over, and where do you see them? You might see the numbers on a clock or watch, or on vehicle license plates, or the grocery store receipt, or your amount of cash back from a purchase, maybe even your hotel room number, and so on. Whenever you receive your special numbers, I encourage you to pause for just a moment. Notice who or what comes immediately into your mind.

It's not unusual for me to awaken from a sound sleep only to gaze at the clock and see 3:33, 3:03 or 3:30. This happens to me especially after I have gone to bed worried about something. The numbers are my comfort and reassurance from my team that all will soon be well again.

Sometimes the numbers that capture your attention are special dates, such as birthdays or anniversaries, or a loved one's time of their birth or their passing.

One of my clients, Celia Cheves Edwards, receives the number 221 every day. She spontaneously awakens during the night to see that the clock says 2:21 am. In the afternoon, her attention is drawn to look at the time precisely at 2:21 pm. This number is significant because Celia's son in spirit, Jeff Rivera, was born on February 21st. Recently Celia shared with me that while she was gambling at a casino, Jeff proved that he was there having fun, too! Celia sent me a photo of the slot machine which showed that her winnings were exactly $221.75. Can you guess the year of Jeff's birth? That's right! Celia's wonderful son Jeff was born on February 21, 1975, or 2.21.75.

Even if you don't know exactly why a certain number seems to be your frequent number, allow yourself to feel comforted when you receive it. Whenever you receive a new number repetitively, I recommend that you trust your intuition to interpret its meaning. There isn't necessarily a one-size-fits-all discernment for the meanings of the numbers that spirit chooses to send us. This is why earlier I recommended that you maintain a journal, so you can identify patterns around when the numbers show up. You are the best-qualified person to interpret the meaning of any signs that you receive. You can trust your own heart.

I have asked my spirit friends whether they enjoy sending us signs, particularly numbers. Their answer is that sending us signs is a double pleasure for the spirits. They enjoy making the sign happen and then watching us receive and recognize it. They feel our excitement as though it is their own!

And what is the spirit world's overall intention behind sending us signs? In a word: love. Your guides, angels, and loved ones in spirit perfectly know your heart. They understand everything that you are happily celebrating or miserably enduring. They are always proud of you, and even more so when you are doing your best in the face of challenging circumstances.

soul smart tip:

Numbers are a playful and happy way for spirit to say: I love you; I am here for you; everything will be all right! Think of repetitive numbers as text messages from Heaven. And when you receive them, say "thank you." Spirit has your number!

CHAPTER TEN

how to have a dream visit

DREAM VISITS ARE A wonderful way to say: "I'm here, I'm doing great, and I love you!" And according to the spirit world, it is possible for any of us to establish optimum circumstances that provide them with the energy boost they will need to come through to us while we sleep.

soul smart tip:

Sometimes a friend or a relative will get the dream visit, or the sign, instead of you. Please let that be okay! Try not to be upset if it happens. Your grief may have been too heavy a barrier, and your loved one in spirit found it easier to get through to the other person with a message for you. Look at it this way: your loved one got through to someone, and both you and the other person received a beautiful gift.

Here is a process that many have found to be successful for inviting a dream visit:

1. Choose one night per week and ask for a dream visit that night.

2. Let your loved one in spirit know. Extend an invitation in your mind. Talk out loud to your loved one if you can, since they enjoy that and it helps to increase the energy between you. Say something like, "(Name), on Sunday night I'm inviting you for a dream visit. Please come!"

3. Remind your loved one daily. "Remember, we have a dream visit appointment on Sunday night."

4. Write your loved one's name on a note. Tape it to your bathroom mirror. Every time you stand in your bathroom, you will see the name and send a loving thought.

5. When the appointed day comes,

    a. Send out lots of thoughts of love and gratitude for that person during the day.

    b. Try to arrange your day so you will have as little stress as possible; although some stress is unavoidable, and that's okay.

6. That night before bedtime, light a candle and meditate. Then place the following items near your bed:

a. A plain glass or bowl of water, because water is a spirit conductor.

b. A picture of your loved one.

c. If possible, a personal item that had belonged to your loved one.

7. Just before falling asleep, focus on a happy memory with that loved one; avoid thoughts that bring pain or grief.

8. Ask for the gift of a dream visit, and ask for the gift of remembering the dream. Ask your angels to help.

soul smart tip:

In the morning, when you first awaken, close your eyes and allow your mind to drift a little. This is the best time to remember your dream visit. If you can't recall that it happened, please let that be fine and don't allow yourself to stress about it: remember that it will happen when the time is right. If you have any memory at all of a visit, write it down or make an audio recording of your experience immediately. And give gratitude! Once you get the dream visit, wait a few months before asking the same loved one for another dream visit. If it doesn't work the first or the second time, just be patient. Try it again in exactly one week, and each week after that, confidently expecting that it will happen when the time is right.

HOW WILL YOU KNOW THAT WHAT HAPPENS WAS REAL?

A dream visit is generally brief and realistic. Your loved one will be instantly recognizable to you, but may appear younger and healthier. The dream will be very compassionate and loving! You may even feel your loved one hugging you. And that special personality and familiar mannerisms will be there, because dying doesn't change anyone's personality.

It is probably only a dream—and not a spirit visit—if the dream goes on and on; the dream makes no sense; it's not like your loved one's personality; or if it feels dark or scary. Your subconscious mind may be trying to work something out. Try again in one week. Remember, your loved one has to practice, so don't give up too easily. Try four weeks in a row before taking time off. Be patient!

soul smart tip:

Now that you know how to create the conditions for a dream visit, be patient. Try it once a week. Don't give up too easily if it doesn't work the first time; try again next week. After you have received your dream visit, don't ask the same loved one again for a few months. And perhaps you will be pleasantly surprised by an unexpected validation instead, such as a sign given through a bird or a butterfly, because your loved one has found another route. Remember to say, "Thank you, that was great! Can you do it again sometime soon?"

—— CHAPTER ELEVEN ——

how to have a meditation visit

WHEN YOU VISUALIZE, OR imagine, having a spirit meeting with your loved one in a special place, you are speaking their language because everything where they are is created by thoughts! Thoughts are the love-language of Heaven. The spirits want us to know that it is easier for them to communicate with us if we will simply close our eyes and think. Remember to mentally recreate the place that both of you most enjoyed. Allow your energy to flow into that place so completely that you can see it, hear it, feel it, touch it, and perhaps even taste and smell it!

In the Hall of Reunion, special guides and angels will assist your loved one in energetically building the place that you are visualizing. When it is ready, the place will be moved onto the astral plane in preparation for your meeting.

soul smart tip:

Make the appointment, including day and time, and invite your loved one. Send daily mental and verbal reminders of your upcoming appointment, including where the meeting will be held. You know how some people say that when they retired, they were just as busy as when they worked full-time? Many of the spirits have said the same thing. Heaven is a lively place with quite unlimited options, and work is like play because you get to do whatever you love to do most. So just the fact that you want to have a visit doesn't mean that your spirit loved one has the time right now to drop everything and meet with you. That is one of the reasons why appointments are so important.

Here is a good example of a meeting place. One of my clients meets regularly with her mother in spirit at an upscale department store. Of course, my client actually is sitting in her meditation space, her living room, but mentally she is located in this ritzy department store.

During the week leading up to the appointment day, she talks out loud to her mother, reminding her of where they will meet. Here is the scenario: she and her mother have just finished a morning of shopping, and they are seated on a lovely sofa in the store, surrounded by their shopping bags. The women are chuckling, heady with the joy of their purchases and the time they've spent together, just the two of them. They hear ambient sounds. The pianist is playing the grand piano, and a sales clerk is chatting with a customer somewhere nearby. They are sitting, smiling, and planning where they will go to lunch. They can smell dark roast coffee coming from the store's café.

My intuition mentoring students often practice creating their meeting places during our sessions together, and sometimes the results amaze me. One time, my client was describing the place where we would meet his grandmother. He said it was his grandparents' living room and he was seated on a couch. At that point, I smelled a delicious aroma. "I detect apples and cinnamon," I mused.

My client laughed. He said, "Granny's in the kitchen making her famous apple raisin strudel. We'll each be having a slice when we meet for our appointment!" Obviously, my client had done a superb job of re-creating the meeting place, and I wasn't surprised when his meeting with his grandmother went very well.

I know you would prefer to see your loved one walk right into the living room and say hello. Unfortunately, that is asking too much. The meditation meeting can take some practice, but it nearly always pays off if the living person is open to it.

GETTING READY

It's a good idea to abstain from alcoholic beverages, meats, and other animal products for at least a full day prior to your meditation meeting, since these things lower your spiritual vibration. You will need to keep all of your thoughts positive, so abstain from scary or violent entertainments and plan ahead to get a good night's sleep.

THE MORNING OF YOUR APPOINTMENT

Do your grounding and protection before you get out of bed, if possible. Remind your loved one by sending the thought that your appointment is today! Tell him or her how grateful you are for this opportunity to meet. When you take your shower or bath, visualize the water as divine white light that washes away any doubt, fears, or energies that could get in the way. Afterwards, pay attention to the products you put onto your body. For example, I use an organic lavender lotion, which is an excellent purifier. You could also take a bath in Epsom salts, but remember to shower off any excess salts afterwards.

HALF AN HOUR BEFORE APPOINTMENT TIME

You may want to light a candle and burn a little sage or frankincense around your meditation space. I play soft music that is meaningful to me. If you can't think of a song, try playing "Somewhere over the Rainbow." I especially like the late Eva Cassidy's acoustical version of this uplifting song. Earlier I mentioned using rosewater. I spray it in the air all around my meditation area and put a spritz of the rosewater on my heart chakra, which is the middle of the chest. **Do you really need to do all these things? Well, they certainly aren't mandatory, but why not use everything that you reasonably can to help raise your vibration? It can't hurt!**

Do your grounding and protection prayer (see chapter 8) and sit in the power (see chapter 9). Use a guided meditation for relaxation if you like. Or sit still and focus on your breathing.

To sit in stillness, it might be helpful to use a visual prompt and mantra. Try imagining one perfect red rose and thinking of the word "rose." All this should take just a few minutes.

ABOUT FIVE MINUTES BEFORE
YOUR APPOINTMENT

It's five minutes before appointment time, and you have done all your preparations. Now you have two options. First, you can "go" to the meeting place five minutes ahead of schedule and wait for your loved one to show. Second, you can use my Love Light Connection technique.

Love Light Connection technique: Visualize or imagine that you can see your loved one as though you are watching him or her in a movie. You can "see" your beautiful loved one completely, from head to toe, looking perfectly healthy, happy, and whole. And now, visualize a beautiful pink light in the center of your chest. **This is the pink light of love and compassion.** Let this pink light expand and fill your heart and lungs. Your pink love light emanates from your heart as a beam of light, traveling all the way from you to your loved one's heart. The two of you are connecting, heart to heart and soul to soul, in this beautiful pink light.

Let that beam of pink light continue to flow. There's no need to think about it; simply let it be. And now, reach out and hold hands with your loved one. If your loved one in spirit is a dog, cat, horse, bird, rat, or other creature without hands, simply hold onto your pet.

Together, the two of you "travel" to the meeting place.

You are there, together now!

Take a look around and survey the scenery. Notice all the little details. Enjoy being in your loved one's company.

Allow yourself to be completely in the moment with your loved one. Accept that the meeting will be brief. Savor it!

And please remember to say, "I love you! See you later." Because we never need to say goodbye.

The pink love light connection technique is included in my meditation, Love Lives Forever: Connect With Your Beloved in Spirit in Appendix F.

soul smart tip:

Some people sense their loved one, but then they might wonder why the loved one doesn't say anything. Perhaps their presence is the message! They are telling you that they love you and they are still part of your life. Try to be grateful for anything you receive. Realize that the connection is usually brief, and be grateful for even a glimpse! Staying in a state of gratitude will raise your vibration and, with practice, your visit can grow more vivid and maybe it will last a bit longer.

Please take a moment afterwards to make note of your experience in your diary or journal. Here I should say that it's helpful to use the Love Light Connection method in conjunction with having an appointment, so that your beloved person or pet will be ready for you!

HOW TO KNOW IF WHATEVER HAPPENS IS REAL

Just as with a dream visit, the proof of the pudding is in the eating. You can trust that it's real if your loved one looks good, is happy, has his usual personality, and the interaction is positive overall. If anything feels negative or "off" about the encounter, then that is definitely not your loved one. It is probably just your mind wandering, meaning that it's time to take a break.

YOUR CONNECTION SHOULD
DEEPEN WITH PRACTICE

You can't just order up Mom and Dad from the spirit world like a burger with fries! Spirit connections can't be *forced* to unfold.
Spirit connections must be *allowed* to unfold.

If you are patient, the payoff can be nothing short of spectacular! Some of my clients who have practiced this technique regularly now receive occasional spontaneous visits from their loved ones, even without asking for them. Their loved ones' faces pop into their minds, and they can sense the presence in a profound and unmistakable way. I have noticed that my students who have these excellent results are the ones with real gratitude, patience, and a go-with-the-flow attitude.

Another way to deepen your connection with the spirit world is to surround yourself with like-minded people. For several years, I've had the good fortune to volunteer with a registered non-profit organization, the Afterlife Research and Education Institute (AREI). I am on the Board of Directors along with AREI president Dr. R. Craig Hogan, Dr. Victor Zammit, and Wendy Zammit. I am currently serving as vice president of the AREI Board and director of mediumship.

AREI hosts low cost or free educational meetings which you can attend from home using free webinar software. Our organization's mission is to support research and education about the greater reality that death is an illusion, and to teach people how to make their own direct connections with their loved ones in spirit. As well, if you'd like to meet in person, there is great news! AREI sponsors an annual symposium in Scottsdale, Arizona that draws hundreds of people. The symposium often sells out in advance. I encourage you to learn more by visiting AfterlifeInstitute.org, which is AREI's website.

MIND-ALTERING SUBSTANCES

Drinking an alcoholic beverage or ingesting marijuana may help some people feel as if they are better opening to spirit, at least initially. But it is far healthier to allow your spiritual connection to build naturally and gradually, in the time and manner that is right for you. A substance that will alter your perception will also impair your discernment, create confusion, and even cause your loved one to break off the connection. You might recall that, way back when I was denying my abilities, I abused alcohol to tune *out*, and not *in*. So please, wait until after your spirit work is done before you have a glass of wine or partake of marijuana. Some people find that they lose their desire for alcohol or recreational drugs as they begin to connect more with spirit.

HEREAFTER NOW: CONNECT WITH YOUR LOVED ONE IN SPIRIT

You may want to try a guided meditation to meet with your loved one. My guided meditation called *Hereafter Now* includes meeting your loved one in a favorite place. I have given you the script in the Appendices. It also is available for purchase on my website, CarefreeMedium.com.

soul smart tip:

Any time you have had a meditation visit, dream visit, sign, or a reading with a medium, please keep it to yourself, except for perhaps sharing it with the one or two people that you most trust. These validations are sacred to you! Don't share them with anyone who hasn't earned your absolute trust.

CHAPTER TWELVE

spirit guides and guardian angels

SPIRIT GUIDES ARE UNSUNG heroes of the Heaven. They work mainly behind the scenes, giving you gentle nudges along your path. They can arrange signs, symbols, synchronicities, and dreams to help to point you on your way. But when you are in the course of exercising your free will, no one on your spiritual team will interfere. That is why it helps to consult with your guides in important situations before you take action. I could write an entire book on spirit guides; but for now, let's get up to speed with the basics.

soul smart tip:

While it may be obvious that we benefit from having spirit guides supporting us, the truth is that the guides need us, too! The relationship between a living person and a spirit guide is mutually beneficial. We are cherished beyond measure and continuously supported by our guides. And without us, our guides might be unemployed. They need to work with us so they can grow and mature in their servant leadership abilities. And anyone who works as a guide will tell you that it's all about being of service!

Your beloved people and pets who have passed can act as helpers, because they love you now and always. However, the majority of spirit guides are not people or pets you know from your current lifetime. Spirit guides have lived many lifetimes, mostly on Earth but not always here, and they have amassed tremendous life experience. Becoming a spirit guide is a process that usually begins with a nomination made to a Council of Guides. The nominated person, or soul, goes before the Council, where he is vetted for the role of spirit guide. **Guides can be male or female. As usual, I use the pronoun "he" for simplicity.** If the soul qualifies for spirit guide training, and if he chooses to be a guide, he will start as a junior guide and work his way up. One day he will become a master spirit guide or a subject matter expert guide.

soul smart tip:

There are different types of spirit guides, including master spirit guides and subject matter expert guides. The guides that are with you right now are there because they are exactly the ones you need!

Subject matter expert guides are those guides who, based upon our current needs, come and go from our teams for a season or a reason. They are specialists who join us and stay as long as they are needed. For example, there are guides who come in and help a pregnant woman through her pregnancy and delivery. There are divorce guides who help until a divorce is completed. If you aren't paying attention to their subtle cues, these specialists will give up and move on. **Subject matter expert guides are in high demand, and they won't waste their time on us if we keep refusing to pay attention.**

soul smart tip:

There is one spirit guide who will never, ever leave you. The master spirit guide is your primary guide. He is with you from birth to death and during your life between lives. Your master guide (MG) is intimately familiar with the blueprint for the life you planned before you incarnated. In fact, your master spirit guide helped you to create your life plan!

Not only does your MG know all about your current life plan, but he is also intimately familiar with all your previous lives, ones in which you came up short and ones in which you succeeded in achieving your goals.

soul smart tip:

Your team is likely to include one or two healing guides. Healing guides are experts who help you to be more compassionate toward yourself and others. True to their name, healing guides will help you to heal yourself and help you to assist in healing others. This includes every type of healing: mental, physical, emotional, and spiritual. A medical professional is likely to have extra healing guides on duty.

When I conduct a reading for a medical professional or primary caregiver, I almost always see a certain symbol, a red cross. This symbol tells me that healing spirit guides are working closely with the sitter. Also, whenever I detect a chronic health condition with the sitter, I know that healing guides are playing a significant role in the sitter's life. Healing guides send signs and synchronicities to help you to choose healthcare providers and discern which treatments are best for you and when.

soul smart tip:

If you do healing work—whether it's traditional medicine, alternative medicine, or energy healing—the healing guides want you to know that they place their loving hands on yours. Their hands help to amplify the universal life force energy and empower the sick to heal themselves.

Earlier I mentioned my healing guide. She is a petite Japanese woman named Wakana. I have given her the nickname "Wi," as she is a wee figure with a powerful energy. Wi first appeared to me in a dream a few nights after I was attuned to Reiki Level One. Later, when I became a Reiki Master Teacher, I developed my classes from inspiration I received from Wi, in addition to the traditional Reiki teachings I received from Natalie Barry, my sister, who is my Reiki Master Teacher. Wi has been known to interrupt me while I am teaching a Reiki class so she can interject a helpful comment. When I was recently hospitalized for a week, Wi never left my side. One of the nurses recognized me and knew I was a medium. She mentioned that she felt "a different energy" in a certain spot in my hospital room. I asked her to point to the spot. The nurse pointed directly to where Wi was standing, even though she was invisible to her.

GUIDANCE QUEST: MEET YOUR SPIRIT GUIDE

If you are ready to get to know your spirit guides, it's a good idea to go straight to the guide who is in charge, namely your master guide (MG). My students have done well using my guided meditation, *Guidance Quest*. I have provided the script in the Appendices, and it is also available for purchase on my website.

Earlier I mentioned that two different mediums independently said that my MG and I had traded places in a previous life. I was his guide, but I was a novice at best, a junior guide in training. I can't tell you how happy I am that I'm in physical form now and L.R. is my guide. He is a highly trained professional guide! He and the rest of my team have explained that everyone meets with spirit guides on a regular basis. You meet with your guides, too, although you may not realize it!

soul smart tip:

You meet with your spiritual team on the astral plane while your body is in delta sleep mode. Each of us has regularly scheduled update meetings to review our progress on our life plans and to discuss potential modifications, challenges, and opportunities. You usually won't remember much about these meetings. It is everyone's intention that your life's path will unfold in the manner that is best for your soul's growth.

YOUR MASTER SPIRIT GUIDE (MG)

I have had the pleasure of empowering hundreds of people to get to know their spirit guides. Even if you have no interest in your guides, please be sure to thank them from time to time and you can skip this part. But if you are ready to meet and work with your guides, keep reading this chapter!

soul smart tip:

Don't get hung up on getting "the one and only correct name" of a spirit guide, because there is no such thing! Remember, spirit guides are at a much higher vibration, where names are unnecessary. But the guides do understand that we don't want to call them "Hey you!" So you and your guides can agree upon the names that you will call them. Simple!

You don't need to get a reading to learn the name of a spirit guide. You can do it yourself. Here's how! After you have done your grounding, protection, and meditation, visualize a blank white movie screen. Ask your master spirit guide, "What name shall I call you?" When a name pops onto your movie screen, then you can say, "I saw the name Pamela (for example). May I call you Pamela?" You will be able to feel whether the name is acceptable or not, and it usually is! If nothing is coming to you on the movie screen, try using a pad of paper and a pen. Write down the name that pops into your mind when you ask, "What name shall I call you?" Then write the name on your paper one letter at a time. Afterwards, say, "I wrote the name Pamela (for example). May I call you Pamela?" Chances are that even before you write the word "yes," you will feel that the name is good. Remember, you're working with a master spirit guide who has had many names in many lifetimes. You just need to hit upon a name that both of you like. It's that easy!

soul smart tip:

Next, you will want to know what your master spirit guide looks like. You can learn what your guide looks like, which is how YOU want to see them and THEY want to be seen, through visualization. You can use your movie screen as a visual tool.

You might also use a guided meditation that is specifically designed to empower you to pick up on the visual appearance of your master spirit guide. It can take two or three times using a guided meditation before you have settled on the visual appearance of your guide.

Now, it's time for us to do the validation exercise! My teacher, Alan Arcieri, passed along this validation exercise to me. Now I share it with my students. It's a lot of fun!

soul smart tip:

Once you have agreed upon a name that you will call your master spirit guide (MG), and you can identify the appearance of your guide, it is time to prove to yourself that this is real and not just your imagination. Ask your master spirit guide to manifest something for you by a deadline date. Two weeks is a good amount of time, but you will likely receive the object sooner. When you choose the object, remember that your MG will use the physical environment around you, so keep your request reasonable.

For example, one of my students asked for a Van Gogh painting as a sign from his MG, not because he was an art aficionado, but simply because the Van Gogh print in my office caught his attention. A day later, an acquaintance posted a photograph of Van Gogh's irises on his Facebook wall for no apparent reason, just to say hello. My student hadn't mentioned the hadn't mentioned the validation exercise to anyone.

Another student, Ashley, received the name "Jeremiah" for her MG during our session. As she later wrote to me, Ashley asked for her sign from Jeremiah by "manifesting one special yellow flower." I should note here, too, that Ashley didn't mention this exercise to anyone. She is a stay-at-home mom whose husband works nights.

Each morning when her husband arrived home from work, their young daughter drew a picture for her father and presented it to him. The pictures were always for Daddy. But on this morning, when Ashley's husband asked his little girl what picture she had drawn for Daddy, her response was surprising. As Ashley wrote to me, "She told my husband, 'Sorry Daddy. But this is just for Mom.'" There on the paper was one large yellow sunflower. The validation exercise with Ashley's master spirit guide, Jeremiah, was completed.

soul smart tip:

Once you have validated that your master guide (MG) is real, you can learn to sense your MG's "yes" and "no" opinions when you ask questions. It takes some practice, but you can train yourself to feel "yes" or "no" as sensations in your solar plexus (middle section) area.

A "yes" opinion from your MG is an uplifting or warm feeling. A "no" opinion is typically a downward or hollow feeling in the solar plexus area.

soul smart tip:

Bear in mind that your spirit guides do not exactly know the future because of free will. But they will happily give you their "yes" or "no" opinions, if only you take a moment to ask.

To get your baseline of "yes" and "no" responses, begin by asking a few simple practice questions to which you know the answers. However, please remember that you are responsible for making your own best decisions! The guides' opinions are intended to help you make those decisions with more confidence and inner peace.

ANGELS AND EXTRATERRESTRIAL BEINGS

I am told that many of the beings we perceive as angels may be higher vibrational beings from other galaxies. There are many galaxies! In 2016, the US National Aeronautics and Space Administration (NASA) revised its estimate of how many galaxies exist from 20 billion to 2,000 billion, and more than 90 percent of these have never been studied. It will not surprise you to learn that there are many places besides this Earth where sentient life exists.

Sonia Rinaldi is a renowned researcher of some 30 years in the area of Instrumental TransCommunication (ITC). Sonia is co-founder and research director of IPATI - Instituto de Pesquisas Avançadas em Transcomunicação, or Institute of Advanced Research on Instrumental Transcommunication. Simply put, ITC is the recording of voices—and capturing of images—of spirits. There are hundreds of documented accounts of conversations that Sonia has facilitated between living persons and their spirit loved ones. One recording that particularly touched my heart was that of a child in spirit who sang her favorite song, from Heaven, for her mother on Earth. Unbeknownst to much of the world—although I suspect not for long—Sonia is now reporting that she has been contacted by friendly extraterrestrials. She refers to these beings as "ultraterrestrials."

I have also spoken with people who have encountered extraterrestrials while sitting in physical mediumship development circles. Physical mediumship is an extremely rare type of mediumship in which the spirit world uses the medium's body to produce ectoplasm that the spirit then utilizes to speak, and sometimes even to materialize. Many physical mediumship development circles sit together regularly for years waiting for even a tiny amount of ectoplasm to finally develop.

In the course of Sonia Rinaldi's work, and during the work of some physical mediumship practitioners with whom I have spoken, the extraterrestrials who made contact, stated that they wish to collaborate with us. It would appear there are extraterrestrials that want to communicate with us, just as much as we want to communicate with our spirit loved ones.

For the first time, I am now publicly sharing that I have a spirit guide who has never incarnated, not even once, on the Earth. He says he is an Arcturian and my master guide L.R. affirms this. My Arcturian guide says that his people, among others, strive to protect Earth from those few extraterrestrials who might do us harm if left unchecked. So far, my Arcturian guide works with me only on occasion when needed.

I am not exaggerating when I say that it took a long time for me to fully accept that I have an E.T. as a guide. I used to be afraid of anything connected with extraterrestrials. In fact, when I was a child playing with the other neighborhood children, I was always the one shooting pretend-aliens with my water pistol.

For most of my adult life, I was interested in UFOs and extraterrestrials, only because of the fear factor. I was fascinated yet terrified of E.Ts. I remember listening to Art Bell on Coast to Coast A.M.'s late night radio show, and then sleeping with the lights on. Little did I know that one day I would have the pleasure of working with George Noory and be a guest on Coast to Coast A.M. and on his TV show. Of course, by then I had become well acquainted with my wonderful guide from Arcturus.

Earlier I mentioned that my Arcturian guide is not always around me. That's because he is a subject matter expert guide. He shows up when I must deal with big challenges and whenever I am working on a project that has the potential to help many people. I think of him as a peaceful warrior who helps to clear my obstacles. In fact, he appears to me wearing partial body armor with his sword sheathed at his side.

Perhaps the next breakthrough in communication between Heaven and Earth will occur due to the assistance of high-vibrational beings who have never even incarnated on Earth. Only time will tell!

soul smart tip:

In the spirit world, you can choose to live in a completely humanoid community and interact only with people like you. Or, you can live in a diverse community where humanoid and non-humanoid beings coexist quite happily. I can't help but think of the cantina scene in the original Star Wars movie! Someday, our happy memories of diversity on the other side will help us to forever end racial discrimination here on Earth.

Years ago, I didn't believe in angels, frankly, because I had never seen one. I saw spirit people and spirit animals, but nothing resembling an angel. I'm a little embarrassed to admit that I used to say, "I'm not really an angel person." Angels seemed too popular. Then finally, one day, I saw an angel for the first time. I was doing my first-ever energy cleansing on our house. Somewhere I had read that you should "ask an angel" to stand in the house while doing an energy cleansing. My left-brained orientation means that I'm methodical, so I called in an angel. Oh my gosh, did I ever get an angel! A moment later, after I had all but forgotten about requesting an angel, to my surprise a ten-foot-tall being appeared in our living room. I heard the word "angel" in a male whisper. The angel had shoulder-length yellow hair, a white robe and white triangle-shaped hat. It had very large arch-shaped violet eyes. There were no wings, but a golden light at its shoulders gave the appearance of wings. Well, at first I nearly fainted. But so much love came over me that I stood transfixed. I wanted to rush towards it, but my feet would not move. Within five seconds, the angel was gone. Apparently I must have needed to see a big angel to get the point!

Since then, I have gotten to know my wonderful guardian angel, Mariella. She has medium-dark skin and long, wavy black hair, and she wears a beautiful sky-blue gown. Yes, my guardian angel looks like a person. A Hispanic female, to be precise! Before every reading when I am opening myself up to spirits I have never met, I introduce Mariella as my guardian who enforces my rules. She does a magnificent job of protecting me. You have a guardian angel, too!

GUARDIAN ANGEL

Every living person has a guardian angel. While other angels come and go, you have an angel who is assigned to you from birth until death just as you have a guide who is constant. One day soon after I had met my guardian angel, Mariella, I asked her what angels are supposed to look like. Mariella patiently explained that the living see angels in whatever way we are open to seeing angels. We pretty much see what we expect to see and what we are comfortable seeing. Mariella said that the angel who had appeared in my living room had scanned my consciousness beforehand and had determined that I needed to see him exactly the way he had appeared to me. That experience opened me up to a whole new area of spirit connection!

soul smart tip:

An angel will scan your consciousness prior to revealing itself to you. The angel will appear, most likely in your mind's eye, as close as possible to what you expect to see. In the presence of an angel, all you will feel is pure love.

To meet your guardian angel, I recommend using a guided meditation or visualization. There are many good ones available online. My *Guidance Quest* meditation in the Appendices includes meeting your guardian angel. Some of my students were recently successful with meeting their guardian angels by using my dream visit method discussed in chapter ten.

THE GUARDIAN ANGEL'S ROLE

People often ask me where the guardian angel was when a person they love was killed. Why didn't the guardian angel save their loved one? My guardian angel, Mariella, has told me why. She used a car accident as an example. Most of us have heard of someone who had a horrific car accident and walked away from it with not more than a scratch. People will say, "Your guardian angel was with you." The reality is that your guardian angel always is with you, from birth until death and between lives.

Someone who walks away from a horrific car accident was spared because it wasn't time for an exit point in that person's life plan. And most life plans have about three potential exit-points, or deaths, built into the plan. If the car accident doesn't coincide with an exit-point, and if an injury wouldn't be in service to that soul's growth or to the growth of someone in that person's life, then the guardian angel's job is to "wrap arms" around the person and cushion his body from harm.

But what is the guardian angel's role if the person really is supposed to die? Mariella explains that the guardian angel would "wrap arms" around the person and take away all pain and fear, and help the soul slip from the body, so that person's soul could then meet a beloved person or pet and cross over to Heavenly home. Remember that death itself is *not* painful, but pleasurable! It is a wonderful experience of light. All our loved ones in spirit are happy, healthy, and whole.

soul smart tip:

In addition to your guardian, you have other angels working with you just as you have several guides on your spiritual team. Your guides are advanced beings who were once in human bodies, while your angels usually haven't had lives on Earth. In general, angels are even more reluctant than spirit guides to interfere with your free will. They hold to the letter of the spiritual law! So please remember to ask for the help of your team, including your angels, even before you need it. A good time to do this is every morning when you brush your teeth. Then you will know that you have asked for their help for the day!

THE UNITY

Remember the bright white light that filled the room whenever my grandfather was writing his sermons? I never thought I would see such a wondrous light again after my grandfather died. But I did! In fact, by now, I have seen this brilliant light many times. And after my near-death experience, the light began to speak to me. I know it sounds wild, even for me, but it is as real as the sun in the sky. The light is how I visually perceive the collective consciousness of very high-vibrational beings who refer to themselves as The Unity. Their mission? To help humankind bring Heaven to Earth.

Since I wrote the first edition of this book, I have been visited by the Unity more frequently. I have now told them that I am ready to let my light shine more brightly. Through the Unity, I have received several healings and teachings. And I can't wait to share more with you soon.

soul smart tip:

It is a privilege to live on Earth, but it is not intended always to be easy! You are cherished and guided by the Source and your spiritual team. No one is loved more than you. Your beloved people and pets in spirit are eager to connect, and happy to help you understand that love lives forever!

And so it is.

appendices

MEDITATION SCRIPTS

———— APPENDIX A ————

meditation:
the daily peace

THIS MEDITATION IS INTENDED to be used every day for grounding and protection. The best time is immediately when you awaken in the morning. Always ground and protect your energy before you open up to connecting with spirits. You are welcome to record yourself reading this meditation script, and then play it back for meditation. Or purchase it on my website, CarefreeMedium.com.

Sit upright in a comfortable chair with both feet on the floor. Yoga students may prefer the half-lotus position, or you may need to lie down with a pillow under your knees to support your back. Let your hands rest in your lap, palms facing up. Close your eyes and mouth and breathe gently through your nose. As you inhale, visualize white light entering your body; as you exhale, let all your breath out slowly, all the way out, breathing in white light, breathing out all stress and anxiety. Letting go, simply being, in the now, the present, this very moment.

Then say, "Divine source, thank you for blessing me with this day, with my life and all my many blessings. Thank you for giving me another day to be of service in this life and in this body. I ask that you cleanse me in divine white light, erasing all energy that does not belong in my auric field. Surround me in a beautiful, translucent golden bubble of protection that is bathed in your divine white light. Sealing in all my positive energies and good health. Sealing out all negative energies, all ill health, all entities from lower realms, and I send white light to the lower realms. So that only peace, love and protection may enter in. I give gratitude for my spiritual team, spirit guides, angels, and my loved ones in the light. I send this light out to each of my loved ones on both the physical plane and the spiritual plane. I send this light out to all those in need of a physical, emotional, or spiritual healing. I connect with universal consciousness. I connect with all beings who are in meditation at this moment. I am eternal. I am one with divine source; I am one with all. Compassion guides all my thoughts, words, actions, and I trust that I will complete my greater work before I transition to Heavenly home. With gratitude and joy, I am a child of God.
And so it is."

—— APPENDIX B ——

meditation: synergy peace manifest health and serenity

THIS MEDITATION IS INTENDED to help you to prepare for connecting with spirit by balancing and recharging your energy centers. You are welcome to record yourself reading this meditation script, and then play it back for meditation. Or purchase it on my website, CarefreeMedium.com.

Begin by choosing the position of your body. It is best to keep your spine straight. You may sit upright in a comfortable chair, with both feet on the floor. Yoga students may prefer the half-lotus position, or you may need to lie down with a pillow under your knees to support your back. Now, close your eyes and mouth. Breathe slowly through your nose. Take a very slow, deep breath in through your nose and then let this breath go out, all the way out, slowly. With your breathing, visualize white light coming in as you inhale. All your tension leaving as you exhale. Take another slow, deep breath through your nose. Breathing in white light, breathing out tension and stress. And now the words of grounding and protection.

"Divine Source, Holy Creator, thank you for blessing me with this day, with my life and with all my many blessings. Thank you for giving me another opportunity to serve you in this body. I ask you to surround me in a beautiful translucent golden bubble of protection that is bathed in your divine white light. Sealing in all my positive energies and good health. Sealing out all negative energies, all ill health, all entities from the lower realms, and I send white light to the lower realms. So that only peace, love, and protection may enter in. I give thanks to my spiritual team, spirit guides, guardian angels, teachers, healers, and loved ones in the white light for their guidance, inspiration, and protection. And so it is."

And now, still aware of your body, relax your neck. Move it slowly from side to side if you like. Let your shoulders drop and your lower back release, letting go. Relax your arms and legs, feeling ever more comfortable.

Visualize, at the base of your seat, a golden cord appearing. This golden cord extends now, going down, through the floor, traveling down, deeply into Mother Earth. Grounding you. Safe and secure. Relaxed and peaceful.

And now, visualize a beam of white light shining down from the sky and entering through the ceiling. You recognize the light and welcome the light like a loving friend. Let this brilliant white light shine upon you, entering your body through the top of your head. Illuminating your entire body, from your head all the way down to the soles of your feet. Brilliant, healing, divine white light. Comforted by the light, healed by the light, restored by the light, in the light you realize that you are so... much... more. You are unconditional love, compassion, and wisdom. You are your gifts. You are one with God. Rest a moment while the light cleanses and restores you. You may be aware of pain in your body. Let this healing light travel wherever you need it most. Healing self in the light... In this divine light, all energy stuck to you that does not belong retreats now. Sliding down to the golden cord below your seat, sliding down through the floor, going deeply into Mother Earth to be neutralized and recycled for future use.

And now, at the base of your spine, the light forms a shining red flower. As the red flower glows, you feel its light cleansing and restoring your root chakra. Your center of grounding, security, and physical intelligence. Replacing feelings of scarcity, anxiety, and worry with perfect trust that abundance and goodness are all around you, in both the physical and spiritual worlds... healed and charged, shining red physical energy.

Rising, the light forms a brilliant orange flower. Two inches below your navel. As the orange flower glows, you feel its light charging your sacral chakra. Your center of emotion, sensuality, and creative intelligence. Renewing desire to live life to the fullest, honor your creativity. Embrace your sensuality. You are creative. You are beautiful. You love life. Life loves you... healed and charged, shining orange creative energy.

Rising two inches above your navel, the light forms a sunny

yellow flower. You feel this yellow flower cleansing and restoring your solar plexus chakra. Your center of personal power, self-confidence, and mental intelligence. Releasing self-doubt. Strengthening discernment, your gut feelings. Awakening the life force within to the universal truth that all things are possible. Healed and charged, yellow mental energy.

At the center of your chest, a flower with luminous green leaves is slowly opening its bright pink bloom. As this pink flower opens at your chest, it begins cleansing and restoring your heart chakra. Your center of unconditional love, healing and empathic intelligence. Opening your heart space to a deeper realization of love all around you, from both the physical and spiritual worlds. Helping you channel universal energy to accept and heal self. Accept and heal others. Filling your heart with peace, faith, and trust. Trust that there is a divine plan. Trust that everything will be all right. Trust that no matter what, you are blessed. Healed and balanced, pink and green empathic energy.

Rising again, the healing light pauses at your throat. Forming a brilliant blue flower. Feel the vibration as the blue flower cleanses and restores your throat chakra. Your center of voice, self-expression, and communication intelligence. Creating clear communication. Opening channel to speak your truth. Take a moment now; speak in your mind all that you need and believe that it will be done. Balanced and healed, clear communication energy.

And now the light travels up to your forehead forming a dark blue, indigo flower. The flower is softly spinning clockwise at the center of your brow, your third-eye chakra. Clearing, balancing, and opening your center of psychic gifts, clear insight and intuition intelligence. Tapping into the power of your soul self. Bringing intuition front and center. Blessing you with the ability to perceive inspiration coming from within and from without. Bringing synchronicities to point the way. Balanced, charged and opened, intuitive energy.

Rising again, the healing light shines at the top of your head, a glowing ray of violet light at your crown chakra. Center of higher self, universal oneness and spiritual intelligence. And now all of the colors join together in a rainbow at the top of your head. Your rainbow is growing and changing. Becoming a vortex or funnel of light reaching up. All the way up, from the top of your head through the ceiling. Into infinite space. Reaching Heaven. Reaching home.

You feel your vibration rising, increasing. Let your mind, let your soul self-flow up through your body, traveling up, free from your body and safely tethered by a thin silver cord. Floating now into the vortex of light. You are with the light. In the light. Of the light. Connecting with your higher self, that part of you that is always with spirit. As you reunite with higher self, you realize you are one with universal consciousness. Complete realization of life. Truth. Beauty. I release the past. I release the future. I live my truth. I release control. I release how others feel. I live my truth. I release fear. I release shame. I live my truth. I live and move and have my being in universal consciousness. All things are possible. All is mine. I trust divine order. I trust there is a plan. I trust I will meet my greater good.

Rest now for a moment. Focus on your breath. Breathing slowly, rest, recharge, and heal. If you would like, you may ask a question or seek guidance. Answers may come from your higher self or your spiritual team. Or simply rest for a little while.

As you float above, look down now at your body. See the silver cord attaching you to your body. Your body has been healing itself. It is time to return. The white light beams down toward your body now, beaming all the way down, through the top of your head to the soles of your feet. Let yourself float with the light back into your body. In your mind say, *"I call my energy back."* You are completely back in your body now. And the light begins to dim, becoming softer and softer. The light fades from view, yet it will never be far away. With your eyes still closed, become more aware now of your surroundings. Feel your body and the furniture where you are seated. Take a slow breath in, and a slow breath out. Completely in your body. Feeling relaxed but energized, healthy and whole. Remember that the peace that surpasses understanding is always available to you. And when you are ready, open your eyes. You are a child of God. You are never alone. Love lives forever. And so it is!

—— APPENDIX C ——

meditation: crossing the threshold preparation to meet with loved ones and guides

THIS MEDITATION IS INTENDED to raise your vibration before meeting with your guides or loved ones in spirit. Use it immediately before *Guidance Quest* (if you wish to meet with your spirit guide) or *Hereafter Now* (if you wish to meet with a loved one in spirit). *Crossing the Threshold* is included at the beginning of both of those meditations available for purchase on my website, CarefreeMedium.com.

Begin by choosing the position of your body. It is best to keep your spine straight. You may sit upright in a comfortable chair with both feet on the floor. Yoga students may prefer the half lotus position, or you may need to lie down with a pillow under your knees to support your back. Let your hands relax in your lap, palms facing up. Now, close your eyes and mouth. Breathe slowly through your nose. As you inhale, visualize white light entering your body. As you exhale, let your breath slowly all the way out. Breathing in white light. Breathing out stress, anxiety, your to-do list. Let go, release, and go to center, to this moment. And now the words of grounding and protection.

"Divine Source, Holy Creator, thank you for blessing me with this day, with my life and with all my many blessings. I am grateful for each day, each opportunity to be of service in this life and in this body. I ask you to surround me in a beautiful translucent golden bubble of protection that is bathed in your divine white light. Sealing in all my positive energies and good health. Sealing out all negative energies, all ill health, all entities from the lower realms, and I send white light to the lower realms. So that only peace, love, and protection may enter in. I give thanks to my spiritual team, spirit guides, guardian angels, and all my loved ones in the white light for their love and support as I walk the path of my life. And so it is."

And now, still aware of your body, let your shoulders drop and relax. Your back is releasing now and feels very comfortable. Visualize below your seat a golden cord appearing. This golden cord extends now, going down, down, deeply into Mother Earth. Grounding you perfectly. And now, still aware of your body, relax your neck. Move it slowly from side to side if you like. Let your shoulders drop, your lower back releasing, letting go even more. Arms and legs relaxed, feeling comfortable. And now, visualize a beam of white light shining down from the sky and entering through the ceiling. Let this brilliant white light shine upon you as it enters your body through the top of your head. Illuminating your entire body, from your head all the way down to the soles of your feet. Brilliant, healing, divine white light. Comforted by the light, healed by the light, and restored by the light.

Think of a loved one in spirit. And invite your loved one to join you in this meditation. Send them loving thoughts. Rest a moment while the light heals you, recharging your spiritual batteries. In this divine light all energy stuck to you that does not belong retreats now. Sliding down through the golden cord beneath your seat, and down through the floor, going deeply into Mother Earth to be neutralized. Visualize that you are standing in front of a large white house. And the front door to this house is open. See yourself walking forward, towards this beautiful house and through the doorway. Notice now that you are standing in front of a long hallway. Look down the hallway, and see there is an elevator at the end of the hall. Slowly begin walking toward the elevator, and notice that there are rooms to your left side and rooms to your right side. Continue walking down the hallway, and as you pass the rooms on both sides of you, each room has a bright light shining through its doorway. A different color light radiates from each room, on your left and on your right. These are healing rooms. And as you walk by them, you can feel the healing energy running through you. Beautiful, laser-like colors. Red, orange, yellow, green, blue, indigo, violet. Feeling very relaxed and peaceful. And now coming to the end of the hallway, the elevator doors are opening before you. Walk into the elevator, turn around, and the elevator doors slowly close. Gently now, the elevator begins to rise, smoothly ascending up, up, slowly.

As the elevator rises, feel your vibration becoming higher and higher. The elevator quietly stops and the doors are opening. Exit the elevator and find yourself in a beautiful room with comfortable furniture. You can choose the color or colors, the texture, fabrics, everything in this room. This is your room. Your sanctuary. Your place to relax, recharge, and heal. Notice in the middle of your room a beautiful, pillowy chair. Go ahead and have a seat in the chair. Feel yourself sinking in, becoming even more relaxed and peaceful. Notice that beside you is a small table with a remote control device. Pick up the remote control, press the button, and as you do, directly across from you, curtains are opening slowly, and these curtains reveal a movie screen. A pure white and pristine movie screen. Put the remote control down on the table beside you and look at the screen. In the center of the screen a small blue dot is appearing. The blue dot is spinning slowly and becoming larger and larger, now filling the movie screen, and morphing, changing into a door, a large wooden door that now fills the screen. And this door has a round golden handle. This is the doorway between dimensions. The threshold to the world of spirit. Now rise up from your chair and walk slowly toward the wooden door. On the count of Three you will pass through the door, over the threshold. One, almost there. Two, reaching out for the golden door handle, holding the handle and pulling it toward you, opening the door, all the way now. And Three, crossing over the threshold.

—— APPENDIX D ——

guidance quest:
meet your spirit guide

THIS MEDITATION IS INTENDED to help you meet with your master spirit guide. You are welcome to record yourself reading this meditation script, and then play it back for meditation. Or you can purchase it on my website, CarefreeMedium.com. When you purchase *Guidance Quest*, it includes *Crossing the Threshold* at the beginning of the recording to raise your vibration.

———————— ❧ ————————

And now you are standing in a garden where every flower is in bloom. Vibrant, colorful flowers, plants, and trees are all around you. Breathe in the sweet fragrances. Feel the gentle warmth of the sun beaming softly on your face. Hear the birds singing. In front of you a butterfly has paused, suspended in the air near your face. See every detail of this butterfly. Hear the flutter of its tiny wings. All of your senses are fully alive and vibrant as you see. Hear. Feel. The butterfly floats downward in front of you, showing you the pathway on which you are standing.

Begin walking on the pathway, slowly. Take in the beauty of this Heavenly garden as you walk. Feeling even more relaxed. Peaceful. Free.

Continue walking, and notice that the pathway is winding around, curving to the right. Follow the pathway as it curves to the right. And now, as you look down the path, notice that there is a lake at the end, a crystal clear, blue body of water. Continue walking toward the lake in this beautiful, relaxing place. Go to the water's edge and look down into the lake. The water is pure, clear; you can see your reflection. See yourself smiling in this reflection, healthy, happy, and peaceful.

And now, there is one who is joining you. This is your master spirit guide, the main guide who is with you all throughout your life, supporting and giving you gentle guidance. This guide is now standing directly at your side and looking at the lake. And both of you are smiling. Notice your guide's reflection in the lake. You may see a color, or colors, an outline or impression. You may see the face of your guide. Don't worry if it's real or your imagination. Simply let it be. And now both of you turn your attention away from the lake, back to the pathway. Begin walking slowly, side by side. And notice, off to the side, there is a park bench under a tree, an enormous tall tree, living here since the beginning of time. The tree of life. Hear the leaves of this great tree rustling in the breeze. The two of you have a seat on the bench under the magnificent tree in this sacred space. Master guide sits beside you, where you will normally find your master guide to be. Sitting, enjoying each other's presence. Let yourself feel your guide's energy vibration. You may notice a sensation in your body, electrical, tingling, or warmth. You may smell a fragrance. Or you may simply know that your master guide is present with you now.

There is another who joins you. A beautiful, luminous angel stands before you now. And this is your guardian angel. The angel who is always with you. Your guardian angel has come to cleanse your energy. With wings of beautiful light, your guardian angel now cleanses your aura, wiping away all energy that does not belong, sending it down into Mother Earth, to be neutralized and recycled for future, positive use. Your guardian angel is repairing your aura, anywhere there are rips or holes, wear and tear that comes with living the human experience. It's okay. You are safe, loved, and healed in this sacred space. And cutting away all negative cords of attachment, helping you let go of that which no longer serves you. And now sealing your aura, protecting it, healthy and whole, so you can hold all the love and light that is your birthright, as a child of the creator. Notice your angel's appearance and vibration, the feelings you receive. You may see a color, or colors; you may see the face of your guardian angel. Don't wonder if it's real or your imagination. Simply let it be. Your guardian angel now smiles. Turns, and steps away. Your guides and angels are gifts from the creator. Remember to ask for their assistance, whenever you feel the need.

Your vibration rises higher and higher. Rest now with your master guide as you sit together on the park bench in this sacred place. You may ask a question or seek guidance. Or simply enjoy each other's company. Take a moment now. And now, you and your master guide stand up. It is time to walk back on the pathway, back in the direction from which you came. As you walk, notice an increased awareness of how the energy of this guide feels to you. Notice which side your guide is standing on. Walking on the path, glance down. You might notice feet, shoes, and clothing. Look up; you might notice colors or facial features. Or simply know, feel, and trust that your master guide is with you now. Continue following the pathway, as you now turn the corner back towards the left. At the end of the pathway, the large wooden door with the golden handle is gently opening. You are almost at the doorway, the threshold back to the room. Turn and face your master guide who is thanking you, telling you, *It is an honor to be of service. You are never apart from the creator, who lives within you. You always have free will, choices to make.*

Your master guide will never tell you what to do, but will gladly give you a gentle nudge, signs, symbols, synchronicities, to help you on your pathway in this life. You shape your destiny, through your thoughts, words, and actions. Being the best "you" that you can be. If you wish, you may thank your master guide, perhaps sharing a hug. Your master guide watches, smiling, as you approach the open doorway. On the count of Three, you will walk through the doorway and find yourself back in your room. One, halfway there. Two, right at the threshold. And Three, crossing the threshold back into your room. Pick up the remote control from the table and press the button. And as you do, notice that the large wooden door on your viewing screen has closed, becoming smaller and smaller, fading away. The curtains are closing as well.

This is your room, your sanctuary, available anytime. Know that you can come back to this place simply by "thinking" yourself here. You can press the button on the remote control, open the curtains, and go through the doorway to the world of spirit whenever you wish. You may use your movie screen to receive images, messages, if you choose. This is your room, your sanctuary, available every hour each day. And now, put the remote control down and walk back to the elevator, as the elevator doors have opened. Enter the elevator, turn around, and see the doors gently closing as the elevator now descends, going down slowly, slowly, and coming to a gentle stop. The elevator doors have now opened. Exit the elevator and start walking down the long hallway to the front door of the house. And this time, as you are walking down the hall, you find that those beautiful lights coming from the healing rooms on your left and right—the lights have intensified.

As you walk by the healing rooms, the lights are supercharging your energy, your aura. Increasing your intuitive abilities. Raising your vibration. Perfect harmony of body. Mind. Soul. The creator's house has many healing rooms. And you can return here. Visit. Anytime. Lie down in a healing room. Relax, recharge, and heal. And now walking down to the end of the hallway, the front door is all the way open. Walk through the front door, exiting the large white house. Now you are walking away, walking away, and walking back to your physical body. With your eyes still closed, become aware of your body. And now, it is time to call your energy back to your body. In your mind, say, "I call my energy back." Become more aware now of the chair in which you sit, feeling the seat and the back of the chair. Take a slow breath in, and a slow breath out. You are completely back in your body now. Very relaxed, yet energized. Healthy and peaceful. Take another slow breath in, and a slow breath out.

Remember, the peace that surpasses understanding is always available to you. And when you are ready, open your eyes. You are a child of God. You are never alone. Love lives forever. And so it is.

—— APPENDIX E ——

hereafter now: connect with loved ones in spirit

THIS MEDITATION IS INTENDED to help you to connect with a loved one in spirit. You are welcome to record yourself reading this meditation script, and then play it back for meditation. Or you can purchase *Hereafter Now* on my website, CarefreeMedium. com. When you purchase *Hereafter Now*, it includes *Crossing the Threshold* at the beginning of the recording to raise your vibration.

And now you are standing in a forest. Lush, green forest. Tall trees all around you. Feel the gentle warmth of sunshine on your face. Glance down at your bare feet, feeling soft, cool grass beneath your feet. Wildflowers of every color of the rainbow in full bloom. Fresh air, the luscious scents of flowers, pine, purity. There is a waterfall off in the distance. Hear the sound of water splashing onto the rocks. Deer are walking through the forest. Hear the soft crunch of leaves beneath their feet.

All your senses are fully alive, vibrant. As you see, hear and feel, continue your walk in this beautiful forest, entering a clearing; now you are standing in front of a small building made entirely of clear, quartz crystal. Walk through the open doorway of this crystal building. Feeling the peaceful vibration. Notice there is no ceiling, no limitations to the light entering in. And now angels join you, floating above. Smiling angels, wings of light. You may see a color, or colors. You may see the faces of your angels. Don't wonder if it is real, or your imagination. Simply let it be.

Your angels are showering you in divine white light. Supercharging your energy with compassion for yourself, compassion for others. Bathing you in peace, joy, trust. Trust that there is a plan. Trust the divine within you. Trust that no one we love is ever really "lost." You stand strong in the light. Connected with the divine consciousness. Absorbing the light into every cell and every atom of your body, so that everyone you meet can see their divinity in your eyes; hear compassion in your voice; feel healing energy from your heart.

One of the angels draws near to you. Your guardian angel, who says, *"Remember to call upon us, your angels. Visit this place whenever you wish. We love you always."* The angels retreat now, floating softly away. But never far from you.

Turn now, leaving the crystal building, back into the forest. In front of you, a hummingbird has paused, suspended in the air near your face. See every detail of the hummingbird; hear the flutter of the tiny wings. The hummingbird floats downward in front of you, showing you the pathway on which you are standing. Begin walking on the pathway, slowly.

As you walk, take in the beauty of this sacred place. Feeling even more relaxed, peaceful, and free. Continue walking. And now, at the end of the pathway, notice there is a lake. A crystal clear, blue body of water. Continue walking toward the lake in this beautiful, serene glade. Go to the water's edge and look down into the lake. The water is pure and clear. You can see your reflection. See yourself smiling in the reflection. Healthy, peaceful, and free.

And now, there is one who is joining you. Your loved one has arrived. Standing directly at your side, looking into the lake. And both of you are smiling. Notice your loved one's reflection in the lake. Happy, healthy, and whole. And now turn, face each other, and embrace. See, hear, and feel this happy reunion. Don't wonder if it is real or your imagination, but simply let it be.

And notice, off to the side, that there is a blanket and picnic basket under a tree, an enormously tall tree, a tree living here since the beginning of time. The tree of life. Have a seat together, enjoying each other's presence, sitting side by side in this sacred place. In coming to this place you are learning to speak the love language of the afterlife. A wondrous syntax of signs, symbols, emotions. Existing on the mental plane. This place is reality. Here. Now.

Your loved one thanks you, and hugs you again.

The picnic basket beside you is filled with happy memories you and your loved one share. Places, events, special moments. As you open the picnic basket, so many happy memories fill your heart with joy. Take a moment, and choose a happy memory of a place that you and your loved one enjoy. You will go to this place, together, in a moment. Perhaps you will choose your backyard, or the beach, a mountain, a hiking trail, a boat, your living room. Any place you both enjoy. Now visualize that place. See it. Hear it. Smell it. Feel it.

On the count of Three, you and your loved one will go to that place together. One, reach your hand out to your loved one beside you. Two, hold hands. And Three, you are both there, together. Completely in the moment. Nothing else exists now. If you would like, you may ask your loved one a question. Or say whatever you wish to say to your loved one. Or simply enjoy each other's company.

Remember that love lives forever. Relationships never end. You are making a new memory, with your loved one, here and now. Sitting together. So much joy.

And now, you and your loved one stand up. It is time to walk back on the path, back in the direction from which you came. Look now at the end of the pathway, the large wooden door with the golden handle is gently opening. You are almost at the door, the threshold back to your room. Turn to face your loved one. Your loved one is happy. Perfect, and doing great and loves you. Always. Your loved one watches, smiling, as you approach the open doorway.

On the count of Three, you will walk through the doorway and find yourself back in the room. One, halfway there. Two, right at the threshold. And Three, crossing the threshold back into your room.

Pick up the remote control from the table and press the button. And as you do, notice that the large wooden door on your movie screen is closing, becoming smaller and smaller, fading from view, as the curtains close on the screen. And now, put the remote control down and walk back to the elevator, as the elevator doors have opened. Enter the elevator, turn around, and see the doors gently closing as the elevator now descends. Going down slowly, slowly, and coming to a gentle stop.

The elevator doors have now opened. Exit the elevator and start walking down that long hallway to the front of the house. And this time, as you are walking down the hallway, those beautiful lights coming from the healing rooms on your left and right—those lights have intensified. As you walk by the healing rooms, the lights are supercharging your energy, your aura. Increasing your intuitive abilities. Raising your vibration. So that you are better able to recognize the signs, symbols, and synchronicities that your loved ones in spirit are sending you all the time. Perfect harmony of body. Mind. Soul. The Creator's house has many healing rooms. And you can return here. Visit. Anytime. Lie down in a healing room. Relax, recharge, and heal whenever you wish.

And now, walking down through the front door, exiting the large white house, walking away, walking away, walking away, and walking back to your physical body. With your eyes still closed, becoming more aware of your body. It is time to call your energy back to your body. In your mind, say, *"I call my energy back."* Become more aware now of the chair in which you sit, feeling the seat and the back of the chair. Breathing through your nose, take a slow breath in and a slow breath out. You are completely back in your body now, very relaxed, yet energized. Healthy and whole, peaceful. Know that you can meet with your loved ones. In your mind, you will prepare the place where you will meet your loved one. See it. Hear it. Smell it. Feel it. Your special meeting place. Sacred space.

Choose the date and the time, and invite your loved one. Sending out thoughts, prayers. The Creator has gifted you with the angels to support you. Your angels are on standby. All you need to do is ask for their help. Take a slow breath in, and a slow breath out. Remember, the peace that surpasses understanding is always available to you. And when you are ready, open your eyes.

You are a child of God. You are never alone. Love lives forever. And so it is

—— APPENDIX F ——

love lives forever: connect with your beloved in spirit

THIS MEDITATION IS INTENDED to help you to connect with a loved one in spirit using the energies of your heart. You are welcome to record yourself reading this meditation script, and then play it back for meditation. Or you can purchase Love Lives Forever on my website, CarefreeMedium.com.

Begin by choosing the position of your body; it is best to keep your spine straight. You may sit upright, in a comfortable chair, both feet on the floor. Yoga students may prefer the half lotus position, or you may need to lie down, with a pillow under your knees to support your back. Let your hands relax in your lap, palms facing up.

Now, close your eyes and mouth. Breathe slowly through your nose. Let all of your breath out, slowly, each time you exhale. Relax, release, and let go.

And now the words of grounding and protection. Divine source, thank you for blessing me with this day, with my life and with all my many blessings. I am grateful for each day, each opportunity to be of service in this life and in this body. I ask you to surround me in a beautiful translucent golden bubble of protection that is bathed in your divine white light. Sealing in all my positive energies and good health. Sealing out all negative energies, all ill health, all energies from the lower realms, and I send white light to the lower realms. So that only peace, love, and protection may enter in. I give thanks to my spiritual team, my spirit guides, guardian angels, and all my loved ones in the light, for their love and support as I walk my path. And so it is.

And now, take in another deep breath through your nose, and release it, slowly.

Visualize or imagine a golden cord appearing below where you seated. This golden cord extends now, going down, down, deeply into mother earth. Grounding you perfectly, calm, and centered. Make sure your body is comfortable. If you like, you may reach out your arms now, and take a nice stretch. Relax, release, let go.

Let the muscles in your back and shoulders soften, and relax. And allow yourself to settle in, beginning to feel very peaceful.

Whenever thoughts float in, there is no need to push them away. Observe the thought as if it were a cloud passing through. Thoughts float by, and simply disappear. Effortlessly.

It feels good to just breathe. And relax, release, let go.

In this peaceful state, you are ready for sitting in the power and the presence of the light. And now, from your solar plexus, deep within your abdomen, a spark of white light begins to appear. This light is your life force energy.

Your light at your solar plexus, begins to grow, and with each breath out, each time you exhale, your light becomes brighter and brighter.

Your light is expanding, from your solar plexus upwards, to the top of your head, and your light is expanding, from your solar plexus downwards, all the way to the soles of your feet. The light illuminates your entire body, so that you are shining from within, and shining from without.

And now take in another big, deep breath, and let this breath all the way out. Above your head, a second light, a much brighter and more intense light, is appearing. This more intense light floats near your head.

In a moment, you will expand your light to merge with the brighter light. With your mind, expand your light now; allow the light inside you to grow, and to fill the room and to merge with the brighter, more intense light above you.

And as you become one with the brighter light, you connect now with all of the unconditional love and compassion in the universe. "The light is unlimited. I am one with the light. Therefore, I am unlimited."

In a moment, you will prepare to make a soul-to-soul connection with your loved one who is in spirit form. But for now, before you make this connection, take a moment.

Think of a place that you and your beloved enjoyed together.

A place you both liked to be, when your beloved was here on Earth. Perhaps you will choose a room in your home, or a park, or a beach; any place where the two of you enjoy time together. Now visualize that place, create a picture of it in your mind. You can see the place clearly, as though you are watching a movie. See it. Hear it. Feel it.

By visualizing the place, you are learning to speak the love language of Heaven. Where all is created by thoughts and feelings. Let yourself, your soul, experience this greater reality. You have prepared the place where you will visit with your loved one.

You are ready now. Your beloved is ready now.

Visualize your loved one, standing before you, appearing healthy, happy, and whole. See the wonderful appearance of your beloved.

Beautiful and perfect, from head to toe, and directly in front of you.

Your heart fills with so much love. A beautiful pink light is appearing in the center of your chest. This is the pink light of love and compassion. Visualize this pink light expanding, filling your heart and lungs with each breath you take. Your pink light is beginning to travel, a beam of shimmering pink light, moving from your heart space, all the way to the heart space of your beloved. The two of you connecting now by a beam of shimmering pink light, heart to heart, soul to soul.

So much love. So much joy. Continue to allow the pink love light to flow, connecting the two of you together. Forever.

It is time, now, for you and your loved one, to travel to the meeting place you have chosen. Reach out to your beloved, hold each other. As you do, the two of you are transported, arriving now, in your special meeting place. Together. So much love. So much joy. It feels good to simply be. Together.

Take a moment now, and enjoy each other's company. If you like, you may speak to your beloved; say what you wish to say. Or ask your beloved a question, and allow yourself to hear or feel the answer. Take a nice long moment together, now, in your special place.

Remember that no one we love is ever really lost. Relationships never end. You are making a new memory now, with your beloved, here and now. A part of your soul has visited your beloved today, and may do so again.

And now, it is time to say "see you later", for there is never any need to say goodbye. Take in a big, deep breath, and exhale completely. Bring your attention now, back to your physical body. With your eyes still closed, become aware of your Earthly surroundings. And in your mind say, "I call my energy back."

Take a slow breath in, and a slow breath out. You are completely back in your body now. Very relaxed yet energized. Healthy and peaceful.

Remember, the peace that surpasses all understanding is always available to you. And whenever you are ready, open your eyes.

You are a child of God. You are never alone. Love lives forever. And so it is.

CPSIA information can be obtained
at www.ICGtesting.com
Printed in the USA
BVHW041727171118
533376BV00015B/436/P